MW00931273

THE SAFETY PIN

Holding Your Life Together
When Its Bursting at the Seams

Dr. Francine L. Hernandez

WESTBOW
PRESS
A DIVISION OF THOMAS NELSON
& ZONDERVAN

Scripture taken from the Holy Bible, NEW INTERNATIONAL VERSION®. Copyright © 1973, 1978, 1984 by Biblica, Inc. All rights reserved worldwide. Used by permission. NEW INTERNATIONAL VERSION® and NIV® are registered trademarks of Biblica, Inc. Use of either trademark for the offering of goods or services requires the prior written consent of Biblica US, Inc.

WestBow Press books may be ordered through booksellers or by contacting:

WestBow Press
A Division of Thomas Nelson & Zondervan
1663 Liberty Drive
Bloomington, IN 47403
www.westbowpress.com
1 (866) 928-1240

Because of the dynamic nature of the Internet, any web addresses or links contained in this book may have changed since publication and may no longer be valid. The views expressed in this work are solely those of the author and do not necessarily reflect the views of the publisher, and the publisher hereby disclaims any responsibility for them.

Any people depicted in stock imagery provided by Thinkstock are models, and such images are being used for illustrative purposes only. Certain stock imagery © Thinkstock.

ISBN: 978-1-4908-7376-3 (sc)
ISBN: 978-1-4908-7378-7 (hc)
ISBN: 978-1-4908-7377-0 (e)

Library of Congress Control Number: 2015904153

Print information available on the last page.

WestBow Press rev. date: 03/13/2015

CONTENTS

Foreword vii
Acknowledgements ix
Introduction xi

I.   Project Runway: What Are You Wearing? 1
II.   The Next Exponential Transformation (NEXT) 10
III.   Being In the Perpetual Presence of God 24
IV.   Breaking Every Chain 33
V.   The Safety Pin 41
VI.   Defying Labels 46
VII.   Jesus' Compassion in our Tomb-like Situations 52
VIII.   Moving Toward Your Purpose 63
IX.   To Midwife My Sister 70
X.   From Pain To Power 75

Epilogue 85

FOREWORD

There is immeasurable confidence in seeing a woman who knows her self worth through God's eyes. When she does not realize the value of who she is in Christ Jesus, she allows the world, her man, family and sometimes her job define her. It is high time that we as women help one another embrace our deep down inside, delicate but strong creation of God! Ourselves! Psalm 139:14 says we are wonderfully and fearfully made and Genesis 1:27 says we were made in the image of God.

The time is now to make a personal decision as to who you are in Christ. Are you fine china, the timeless, delicate work of art, cherished and proudly displayed, or are you flimsy, weak, disposable, replaceable and soon discarded as in a paper plate? Are you recycled paper or are you the best glass money can buy? Are you a one of a kind design, patterned after God, or are you a cookie cutter mold, patterned after life's circumstances?

If you have been searching for an insightful and Biblical based guide to God's view of you, search no further. "The Safety Pin" is for you. Francine L. Hernandez provides the reader with strategies, prayers, scriptures and testimonials that are inspiring, encouraging and compelling women to rock the world! Not for self-elevation, but for the building of God's Holy Kingdom. Warmth and transparency are two attributes she shares as she talks to the reader as a best girlfriend.

I recommend a cozy chair, a warm throw, a cup of tea, and a box of tissue as excellent companions as you open page after page, this gift called "The Safety Pin."

Dorrie Adolph
Executive Vice-President
John R. Adolph Ministries
Beaumont Texas

ACKNOWLEDGEMENTS

The idea for this book evolved around several conversations with my sister, Aseelah Monroe, who knew my story and encouraged me to write it so that it could be a blessing to other women.

Thanks to the "I'm Just Saying Women Retreat" facilitators: Rev. Christine Bridges, Dr. Leslie Duroseau, Rev. Denise Parker Lawrence, and Dr. Lillian Reynolds, who believe in my vision for helping women to get in touch with their narratives and held me to the task of writing this book.

Thanks go to my husband, Luis Hernandez, who gave me space to write during the late hours of the night and believed in my ability to complete this task.

And thanks to my children, Brian, Christi, and Jason, who kept me encouraged.

I dedicate this book to the memory of my mother, Foye Suggs, who taught me the importance of having a personal relationship with God.

INTRODUCTION

The self is a world unto itself; at times the inner
world of the self becomes disoriented, disorganized,
disillusioned; in that moment we feel as if we are
falling apart, 'a safety pin' is given to hold us together.

Our Truth

At times we may find ourselves searching for the truth
about our purpose and our destiny. We may be forced to
align ourselves with other people's definition of what and
who we are supposed to be. The journey toward the truth
about our identity is filled with distress, discouragement,
disappointment, and disillusionment, yet I contend here that
those are the dynamics in our lives that strengthen us. These
dynamics shape and configure us into the beautiful "Living
Human Document"[1] God intended us to be. The navigation
system of our lives has already been programmed for our
destination. But many times, family dynamics and life's
distractions have interfered with the frequency needed for
optimal spiritual growth and development.

---

[1]   Robert C. Dykstra, *Images of Pastoral Care: Classic Readings* (St.
Louis, Missouri: Chalice Press, 2005), 22.

Some of us may suffer from a lack of self-efficacy; we fail to believe in our potential. However, I believe that you hold the power to change the landscape of your life, and you can carve out a new 'you' and bring about a desired outcome."[2] God has given us grace enough to walk providentially toward our fullest potential. We have to take our power back and celebrate that victory.

Beginning of the "I'm Just Saying Women's Retreat"

Many times we have made decisions that have caused labels to be placed upon us. I began doing women's retreats four years ago. God inspired the title "I'm Just Saying Women's Retreat." The name of the retreat has meaning. It suggests that women are saying something, and they need to be heard. They often express the pain in their hearts through action or attitude. They may express their joy through loud adoration or through the tenderness of a tear. Their voice seeks that place where their words have value and are validated. Therefore, these yearly retreats not only give space for women to share their inner-worlds of conversation, but the aim is to help women identify issues and prepare a path for appropriate interventions. My facilitators and I want to hear women's stories, withholding our judgment and listening empathically.

We believe that each of us has our own narrative, and within the themes and red threads of our story are the resources that will help us with next steps forward. During these retreats, we extend the opportunity for women to

---

[2] Calvin S. Hall, Gardner Lindzey, John B. Campbell, *Theories of Personality* 4th Edition (Canada: John Wiley & Sons, Inc.) 608.

reveal their ugly realities or celebrate their present victories. Many times these 'realities' are draped with high fashion and expensive cosmetics, and the current popular shade of lipstick. Or they may hide their joy because they fear that other women might reject them. In other words, there are hurting women who dress up beautifully, but the outer garment is only a cover-up for the inner pain. And there are those who may hide their beauty because of fear of not being accepted.

During the last ten years of training ministers, seminarians, and laypersons in Clinical Pastoral Education, I have been privileged to research and study various personality theorists. Within the tenets of these theories, there are kernels that have helped me to understand human development and people's personalities. Studying these principles changed my posture of how I relate to others. Prior to my training in Clinical Pastoral Education in tandem with learning the various personality theories, I was rather quick to pass a judgment on a behavior, or make assessments on people's interactions with me and others. I learned through my research that family and cultural dynamics shape people. The person in front of me has a story, and that story is written upon the lines of their lives and played out in attitudes, values, assumptions, and beliefs. In order to better understand a person, I learned that I needed to engage them and hear their story without presuppositions and/or coloring the story through the lens of my culture, my beliefs, or my traditions, which may be fraught with biases.

One such theory of personality is Maslow's Hierarchy of Needs theory. Maslow lists the need for 'safety' as the second most important need that a person has. "These include security, stability, dependency, protection, freedom from fear, need for structure, etc."[3] Though here he references safety as it relates to the need to feel physically secure, I suggest here that the need extends beyond the physical need of security to the need to feel emotionally secure. One needs to feel safe about knowing that inward feelings and internal thoughts can be shared openly and honestly in an environment that offers unconditional positive regard. Carl Rogers says, "If an individual should experience only *unconditional positive regard*, then no conditions of worth would develop, self-regard would be unconditional..."[4] Women need space to express themselves freely, and feel the acceptance of those who dare listen.

A word to the wise, sister; I contend that if you would only seek to learn and then accept your sisters' internal dynamics as you do her external posture, you would liberate her in unimagined ways. By virtue of your 'hospitality'[5] you will contribute to her unparalleled growth. The blessing of sisterhood is having other shoulders to lean on. Inherent in that relationship is the comfort of warm hospitality. But you cannot offer it to others without first offering it to yourself. Henri Nouwen writes poignantly about the nature and nurturing qualities of hospitality. He says, "Paradoxically, by withdrawing into ourselves, not out of self-pity but out of humility, we create the space for another to be [her] himself and to come to us on [her] his own terms."[6] Offering hospitality to yourself will enable you to offer hospitality to

---

[3] Calvin S. Hall, Gardner Lindzey, John B. Campbell, "*Theories of Personality*" (Canada: John Wiley & Son, Inc., 1998) 449.

[4] Ibid, 467.

[5] Henri Nouwen, *The Wounded Healer*, (New York: Image Books Doubleday: 1990) 89.

[6] Ibid, 91.

another. In essence, the same power that frees you will release your sister.

Many of the women I have encountered on the journey have so desired to be authentic, but felt the "safety net" would not be there. So they have resigned themselves to wearing masks. Wearing masks has become the order of the day. If the truth is told, you may not have been introduced to the sister that you hang out with on occasion; that you sit next to in the church. The sister you laugh with at sorority gatherings, or even pray with in women's groups—unless, of course, you have offered her hospitality, and a sacred space to *be*. You may have only met the person that is socially accepted, or the woman with whom others can feel comfortable. You may have only touched upon the mask on her face. Yes, you may have only seen her persona. "The persona is a mask adopted by a person in response to the demands of social convention and tradition...the purpose of the mask is to make a definite impression upon others and it often, although not necessarily conceals the real nature of the person."[7] The mask can become so real that we begin to identify more with the mask than our real selves. The ego begins to identify with the persona so much so that, according to Jung, "the individual becomes more conscious of the part that he [she] is playing than he [she] is of his [her] genuine feelings."[8]

Your sister, your fellow worshipper, may be forced to abide in the clandestine darkness of self-shame. I believe that women want to be free to be themselves! Your sister may long to express her pain, long to cry on your shoulder. Maybe you need a shoulder to cry on, a place to drop the mask and be transparent. We need to offer space for each other. We

---

[7] Hall, 88.
[8] Ibid, 89.

should throw a "Mask" party. Not a costume party, but a mask party, where women can wear the masks that best reveal the person they are on the inside. At that party, allow the women to share why they wore a particular mask, and how they identify with that mask. The party should not be shame-based, but grace-filled. And then, get this, at the end of the party, burn that darn mask! And celebrate a "Real Me" coming-out party. This would be the kind of celebration where women would be free to experience the joining of the private self with the public self and living out loud!

Allow me to make a disclaimer here; I am not talking about all women, because there are those who thrive in the freedom of being. There are some of you who offer extensive hospitality. You couldn't care less about what others think or even believe. My hope is that this kind of freedom extends to your sisters who have yet to discover the type of liberation that allows them the expression of being what God has already ordained. "For in Him we live and move and have our being" (Acts 17:28 NIV). It is the *being* that needs more expression!

Hopefully, this book will help women to begin or continue the process toward their best being. I hope you are encouraged to know that where you are right now is only your transfer station. It is not your destination! Your destiny is tied in the being that God has already ordained for you. The transfer station is only a place in which to pause and make determinations as to which direction would lead to discovering your truth; not the ones that have been told to you or passed down through generations. Truths have the power to break generational patterns and cycles. I hold these truths to be self-evident; that women search for the means to differentiate not only from family secrets, but also from experiences that brought pain.

So these retreats are geared toward addressing some of the labels, some of the pain, and some of the barriers that prevent women from reaching self-actualization: "the desire to become more and more what one idiosyncratically is, to become everything that one is capable of becoming."[9] They are designed to free the joy within. The various themes of each retreat focus on areas of women's lives that may have caused them to not be destiny-driven. They are designed to give women the opportunity to traverse the internal terrain of their lives and discover lost power and lost opportunities, to encounter and embrace their destiny.

Being a certified Clinical Pastoral Educator for more than ten years with the College of Pastoral Supervision and Psychotherapy, I have trained students/trainees who were transformed by their increasing awareness of self. The pivotal moment was accepting the self, with all its ugliness and its beauty. Integration brought empowerment. They were able to disclose their struggle with shame issues and their desire to make sure the shame did not become toxic. The students/ trainees valued the opportunity to process such shame issues in safe environments that perpetuated "Recovery of Soul" (CPSP Covenant). "Toxic shame, the shame that binds you, is experienced as the all-pervasive sense that I am flawed and defective as a human being...Toxic shame gives you a sense of worthlessness, a sense of failing and falling short as a human being. Toxic shame is a rupture of the self with the self."[10] One of my goals with students that I have trained or with persons I have counseled is to empower them to remap, re-author, and re-assess any shame narratives through the lens of self-love.

---

[9] Calvin S. Hall, p. 450.
[10] John Bradshaw, *Healing the Shame That Binds You*, (Deerfield Beach, Florida: Health Communications, Inc.) 10.

As a Clinical Pastoral Educator, I want to help students increase self-awareness and interpersonal awareness. The focus is always on the self. Students leave the CPE program better able to minister to others because they are more aware of their personhood, and better able to use their weaknesses as strength. They understand how their personal issues hindered them from ministering effectively to members within their churches. There were ministers who wanted to avoid counter-transference (Freud) and the working out of their issues on their congregants or family members. These kinds of engagements with ministers and laypersons who trained with me were pivotal in my discernment of the kind of approach to take with each IJS Women's Retreat.

The ultimate goal of my role in the helping profession is to help cultivate a 'whole' self, a self that holds the reflection of Christ himself. Jesus takes all of us and makes the best of us. Hopefully reading this book will yield a better you, one primed for your purpose, and determined to reach your destiny. Some of the chapters in this book are named after the themes of the first four retreats of I'm Just Saying Women's Retreat.

Facilitators of I'm Just Saying Women Retreat

Surveys from the retreats revealed the blessings that women received. I am privileged to have four facilitators who worked diligently to journey with women who attend these retreats. Rev. Christine Bridges[11] utilizes the candy Skittles, where

---

[11] Rev. Christine Bridges is an ordained minister with the African Methodist Episcopal Church. She is a nurse manager with Visiting Nursing Services of New York. She is a chaplain resident.

she explores some of the paths women may have chosen. She uses this assortment of flavors/colors as a metaphor for the assorted life experiences and interpersonal relationships that women have. Rev. Bridges helps the women who attend her workshop to "rediscover the sacred rhythms of memory making and rituals that bring meaning to their lives." She honors both the similarities and differences of women. She thus encourages women to embrace who they are.

The Skittles exercise is one that allows the women to enter into a process of looking at a bag of candy with a new perspective. For instance, if one of the women in her seminar chooses a yellow Skittle, she invites them to talk about moments in their lives when they felt the sunshine, joy, or happiness. She asks the women to think about the role they may have played in not experiencing joy. She examines some of the attitudes that might serve as barriers to joy. Ultimately, she challenges them towards ownership of the various dynamics of their lives.

Dr. Leslie Duroseau[12] has been a liturgical dancer for over 20 years. Her dance seminar is a paradigmatic shift in how we experience God. It is not about simply dancing as one might do in the dance ministry; it is about seeing one's life as a dance with God. She helps women recognize the different dances they are called to engage in. Dancing is joyful, and no matter what you are going through, if you can dance like no one is watching, you just may enter that space where God has invited you to experience a different kind of intimacy.

Dr. Duroseau asks the women, "Why dance?" She helps women realize that dance has the power to shift the

---

[12] Rev. Dr. Leslie Duroseau is the Senior Pastor of a United Methodist Church in Hampton, New York, and a liturgical dancer for more than 20 years.

atmosphere, and change the women to explore new levels of being with God. Why dance? Dance allows for the freeing of one's soul. Dance is an expression. Dance is truth. Essentially, Dr. Leslie helps women view their lives as a musical piece that God has been working on since their conception. Many of the women leave the retreat with a different melody playing upon the instruments of their lives, upon the strings of their hearts.

Rev. Denise Parker Lawrence[13] has designed her seminar to help women look critically and reflectively at the issues that have placed them in a maelstrom of operating at a less than optimal level. She invites them to pause during the two-day seminar to sit with themselves long enough to discover those biases that keep them in strained relationships with other women, and even in their relationship with significant others. More importantly, Rev. Parker Lawrence's seminar helps women map their lives through a genogram that gives them a three-generational view of their family system. She further joins them in recognizing and breaking negative patterns in their lives. Women leave the seminar more determined to walk the path of least resistance to the commands and dictates of the Lord.

Rev. Dr. Lillian Reynolds'[14] seminar is entitled "Grace, Peace, and Purpose." The seminar's ultimate intent is to help direct women toward God's plan for their lives. She helps the women initiate the process of forgiving themselves for the hurt to themselves and the pain they have caused others. One important concept that I encouraged Dr. Lillian to keep in

---

[13] Rev. Denise Parker Lawrence is an ordained minister at Allen Cathedral in New York. She is a Certified Chaplain and a Certified Pastoral Counselor.

[14] Rev. Dr. Lillian Reynolds is a social worker and the director of Freedom Schools.

her seminar is the sacred moment of helping women to "Get in Touch With the Little Girl within Themselves." She often brings detailed and colorful pictures of little girls and asks the women to share their thoughts and feelings as they reflect on particular images. During this exercise, several feelings are evoked as they think about their childhood, with all its pains and joys.

Dr. Lillian says to the women, "Although we have grown up to be beautiful women, there is still a little girl inside each of us. For some of us, that little girl has been lost, hiding under the suppression of and oppression of someone else's expectations."

As Dr. Lillian focuses on discovering one's purpose through the power of God's grace, she also leads the women toward recognition of how the demands of life, family, work, and careers can keep them from being all that God has called them to be and to do.

These retreats are an intimate gathering of women. Essentially, IJS Women's Retreats were pivotal in my decision to write this book and help women move to the place called intimacy with self and with other women. Facilitators allow the themes I choose for each retreat to serve as an umbrella under which to design their seminars without changing the basic tenets of their seminar. The finale that I present culminates the persuasion of the theme.

In the first four chapters, the themes of each retreat fill the pages, and hopefully will fill your heart with enough experiential process that a fullness of possibilities becomes yours. You are special to God. You are a benefit of God's goodness, a recipient of renewed mercies, and a receptacle of continuous grace. You no longer have to be chained to the pain of your past or the mistakes of your present.

Brief Introduction to the Chapters in the Book

The title of the first chapter is: "**Project Runway: What Are You Wearing?**" This chapter focuses on the many attitudes that we have that keep us living beneath the privileges that God has given us, and far from the scope of being holy epistles. Hopefully, you will recognize these emotions as something that prevents you from being, and reaching a place of total surrender. Once you understand the tactics of the enemy, you will become better equipped to be a "good soldier." You will become more aware of the power you give away to an enemy who is determined to keep you out of fellowship with God.

Chapter 2: **NEXT: Next Exponential Transformation!** This retreat helped to propel women into a closer walk with God by virtue of their preparation to enter the Holy of the Holies. *I contend that women need to be intentional about positioning themselves to stand humbly in the presence of our God.* Too many of life's distractions interfere with making time to be with God. He is Holy, and it is a privilege and an honor to worship at His throne. And though our humanity seems empty before His divinity, His love fills us just the same. We stand in the saturation of love and know that we belong. One must have the proper posture to enter the Holy of Holies, and to step into the next exponential transformation. There is no measuring it. It expands beyond quantitative value. There is that place in our journey where only the transformed dare enter. In this chapter, women are invited to move out of the outer courts of living and into the Holy Presence of God. In order to enter the Holy of the Holies, she must follow a particular process. Here we deliberate on that process, and usher her into that place where breakthroughs are a natural occurrence.

Chapter 3 is entitled: **"Being in the Perpetual Presence of God."** We learn to reshape our lives in such a way that each moment is a time with God, even when we feel that God is nowhere around. We begin to understand that God's presence permeates every circumstance of our living and breathing. There is that knowing and honoring His strength, even in our weakness. There is that basking in His light even in the scariness and discomfort of our darkness. The dynamics of this retreat also focus on the brokenness in the lives of women, and how by women addressing the pain of their lives they would perchance help other women embrace the seeming disintegration in their lives. Together women can tap into power they did not know was available, and thus help their sister to tap into her power.

Chapter 4 is entitled: **"Breaking Every Chain."** Within us, there is power to begin the needed process of dealing with every link in the chain that seeks to bind us. Many links to our past have caused us to live a life of bondage. Jesus wants to set you free! I briefly share some details about the woman of Luke, chapter 13 who had dealt with a "chain" for 18 years. I write about the moment she stood in the presence of God and listened to His words, "Woman thou art loosed from thy infirmity" and the beauty of her chains falling off. Yes, her chains broke, and she was no longer bent by the bondage of her circumstance. Perhaps her story resembles your story. I likewise hope her miracle will be yours.

When I was a child, I discovered the power of faith and hope in God who cares about the smallest things that concern me. I share how my faith journey started with a safety pin. So, chapter 5 bears the name, "**The Safety Pin**" which is also the title of this book. This chapter gives the reader a glimpse into my personal life of faith, and how the safety pin became a symbol of hope, of trust, and of a blessed assurance that God is ever near, ever caring, and ever bringing me to my purpose. Hopefully, you too will discover your own safety pin, and even more so, rediscover your faith journey.

Chapter 6 is my personal invitation to women to remove the labels that we place on other women. Thus it is entitled: "**Defying Labels.**" We owe each other a chance to hear the other's story and the evolution of those stories. My story of yesterday may not be my story of today, and if you remember the details of my past, you might just miss the miracles of my present. I revisit the story of Martha in an effort that you might notice a sharp turn that Martha made that is opposed to her being labeled a worrier. Her kitchen story is filled with distractions, demands, and seeming defiance toward her sister, Mary. Her distractions with food took her attention from what was important at the moment; it further caused her to make demands of Jesus to make her sister codependent in her distractions. Even sadder, she seemed angry with her sister, and outright defiant. But read chapter 6 and fall in love with Martha. Or perhaps see the 'worrying' Martha and the 'faith-filled' Martha in you.

Chapter 7 is entitled: "**Encountering Jesus in Our Dark Moments.**" It takes us to a story in Mark 5 about the demoniac. Here, I again address how labels are placed on people and the genesis of such labels, and how people are seeking freedom from the things that try to bind them. I share the power of Jesus' compassion and His power to transform. What is key in this chapter is the graphic demonstration of

Jesus' command over the darkness that seeks to demand our very soul.

Chapter 8 is entitled "**Moving Toward Your Purpose**." I reflect briefly on Viktor Frankl's book *Man's Search for Meaning*, and how he found the wherewithal to keep going by staying focused on his desire and hope. Hopefully, this chapter will call you to a higher level of thinking about purpose and destiny and meaning making. What is it that holds the center and core of your life? What is your reason for being? Discovering your life's meaning will have a profound impact on how you navigate the terrain of doubt when you experience what seems to be the very absence of God.

Chapter 9: **To Midwife my Sister**. In this chapter I challenge women to entreat other women as if they were pregnant and about to give birth. I challenge women to recognize the delicate moments of your sister's life. To walk with her as if they were experiencing their own labor pains and were in need of someone to help them push forth their destiny! We need to recognize labor pains in our sister. Sometimes her negative attitude can be the result of labor pains. Recognizing the look of travail may call you to walk a journey with your sister as she calls her purpose by name!

Chapter 10: "**From Pain to Power**." I share a true story of a woman who was raped at the age of 12, and how she garnered the strength to accept her beauty even though an ugly attack threatened to take away self-esteem and self-worth. This chapter gives you an intimate view of her pain and how she experienced the pain yet refused to give the pain power over her life. Her forgiveness propelled her to move on, complete high school, college, and graduate school, and she excelled at the top level in her career. At the end of the book, I share with the reader one of my favorite sermons of empowerment. I pray that reading this book will help you to move to a place of carving out a new sense of self, a self that is labeled by what God calls you: "My beloved daughter!" I further pray that you will discover, or rediscover, what it means to have your very own "Safety Pin."

CHAPTER ONE

Project Runway:
What Are You Wearing?

On the runway of your life, what outer garments give definition to who you are? Is it your makeup that defines you? Is it Ruby Woo? Is it Mac, Fashion Fair, Chanel, or the less expensive makeup you can purchase at Walgreens? Perhaps it is the St. John's dress, the Louis Vuitton purse, the Christian Louboutin shoes, or even the off-the-rack gorgeous blouse you recently bought for $29.99 that makes you feel and look like a million dollars? All of this, whatever the price, can easily be called the pseudo-covering of a pain-filled life, the beautifying of an otherwise ugly reality.

I invite you here to consider attitudes and decisions and choices that have covered you. Consider the beauty that Christ has designed for you and is hidden behind your negative response to hurt, pain, and life, when life does not deliver according to your expectations.

Many times our lives are lived in a vortex of negativity. The negative can come from what we have not done, as well as what we have done, and from what others have done to us. For instance, if someone who you thought should have

1

loved and protected you has hurt you, you may go down the runway of life with the garment of unforgiveness.

John Patton writes his thesis expressively on forgiveness:

> "[Human] *forgiveness is not doing something but discovering something-that I am more like those who have hurt me than different from them, I am able to forgive when I discover that I am in no position to forgive. Although the experience of God's forgiveness may involve confession of, and the sense of being forgiven for, specific sins, at its heart it is the recognition of my reception into the community of sinners—those affirmed by God as His children.*"[15]

Forgiveness is always something you do for yourself, and something you do with the realization of your need for forgiveness. What stands out most is that it helps you to acknowledge and cherish the awesome awareness that when we forgive, it is because we know that forgiving identifies us as those who have been received into a community that includes all forgiven sinners on whom God has placed his blessing.

Listen, my sister; when we do not forgive, we are wearing clothes from another (woman's) person's closet. If someone hurts you, then hurt was in his or her closet. People cannot give you what is not already hanging in their closets. "Hurt people hurt people," says Dr. Sandra D. Wilson. And then we carry that hurt into a garment of unforgiveness. Make a decision today to go on a shopping

[15] John Patton, *Is Human Forgiveness Possible: A Pastoral Care Perspective* (Abingdon Press: Nashville, 1993) 16.

spree and find clothing that resembles the light of Christ. "Rather, clothe yourselves with the Lord Jesus Christ, and do not think about how to gratify the desires of the flesh" (Romans 13:14 NIV).

Forgiveness is a process. Begin with acknowledging that the pain you feel is because of what was done to you, and it will not define you. Make up your mind today that you will not borrow from, buy from, or even accept the garments from another person's closet.

When Jesus said to his Father, "Forgive them for they know not what they do" (Luke 23:34), he was offering you and me an insight into others. People who hurt you do so not knowing you, not knowing your purpose, not knowing your history or your family dynamics. They hurt you because they are hurting. So, what you forgive many times is their lack of knowledge. You forgive their unresolved issues. Forgive it feels good and it wears well!

Wearing God's garments

God desires "to bestow on [us] a crown of beauty instead of ashes, the oil of gladness instead of mourning, and a garment of praise instead of a spirit of despair" (Isaiah 61:3). The garments that many of us wear are the reflection of experiences that occurred in our lives, and we have allowed the enemy to define us by those experiences.

Years ago, I counseled a young lady who had contracted HIV/AIDS. Her story moved me to tears, but at the same time inspired joy.

The framework of these sessions explored her story and next steps. As she shared her story, it was not about contracting AIDS; it was about the glory of God. She refused to concentrate on what she called "the things I cannot change," so she focused on what lay ahead. Even as she shared a story about almost being raped and having to run away naked in the woods at night, she kept saying, "It was the grace of God." She did not share anger and blame. She saw her escape as the hand of God on her.

In one session she wanted to sing a song "I'm gonna stay right under the blood, I'm gonna stay right under the blood, I'm gonna stay right under the blood and the devil won't do me no harm." What I learned from this young lady was that she had refused to wear the spirit of despair, and chose rather to put on a garment of praise. She even forgave the person who infected her with the AIDS virus. And she forgave herself.

As you reflect on the various stations of your life, which garments are you still wearing? Did someone hurt you years ago and you are still wearing unforgiveness? Being unforgiving is like wearing fifty-pound stilettos. Forgiving is one of the most freeing experiences you can have. "Therefore I tell you, whatever you ask for in prayer, believe that you have received it and it shall be yours. And when you stand praying, if you hold anything against anyone, forgive him, so that your father in heaven may forgive you your sins" (Mark 11:24–26).

We all have differences among us from time to time because we all have imperfections and at times, sharp tongues. It is only through the grace and mercy of God that we are able to walk through our failures. If you have unforgiveness in your heart, it will affect you. It will negatively impact your relationships—with God, with one another, at church and on your job. It will certainly diminish your sphere of influence.

Envy/Jealousy

"Anger is cruel and fury overwhelming, but who can stand before jealousy?" (Proverbs 27:4). When Rachel saw that she was not bearing Jacob any children, she became jealous of her sister; so she said to Jacob, "Give me children, or I'll die!" (Genesis 30:1). Rachel wrapped all of her hope for living in having a child for the man she loved. For the Hebrew women, being barren was one of the greatest misfortunes that could befall them.[16]

Rachel's worth was tied to what she did, and not to who she was. Where is your worth? If I asked you to say who you are, would you describe your 'doing' or your 'being'? Would you describe your character or your career? In other words, would you offer a list of the things that you do, such as mother, wife, teacher, nurse, etc., or can you reach into your heart and take hold of your essence. Your essence is the thing that shapes your being, such as giver, listener, change agent, visionary, etc. It is that which drives, motivates, and moves you toward your purpose. Rachel was given a description by the society and culture that she lived in; it was one where if you did not have a child, then your worth as a woman was diminished. She was trapped in a culture that did not value individuality. The value was place on expected norms; women produce children.

During the times that Rachel lived, a woman's worth was in her ability to give a man a man-child. Worth was externally placed upon them. So, when Rachel did not conceive, while Leah was continuously having children, she became jealous and envious. She wanted to live out the

---

[16] (Ellicott's Commentary for English Readers on Gen. 30:1)

dictates of the external world while her inner world began to crumble. She was so blinded by such dictates that she failed to embrace and cherish the love that Jacob had for her. Rachel's attitude was detrimental and destructive to having a cordial relationship with her sister. Wasted time—time that she could have experienced intimate moments with her sister was lost on competitiveness. What about you? Have you wasted time being jealous when you could have spent time getting to know your sister's story, her pain, and her joys?

We should thank God for what we do have and refrain from complaining about what we do not have. If you surveyed the blessings that God has given you, you would soon discover that you owe God, and God has been good to you. Our focus should cause us to develop relationships with our sisters, not destroy them. Rachel was blinded by her insecurities. She did not have power from within to own who she was. I am not sure what she saw in the mirror, because Scripture says in Genesis 29:17: "Leah had weak eyes, but Rachel had a lovely figure and was beautiful."

Erik Erikson's eight stages of development include *intimacy vs. isolation.* "A prerequisite to establishing this intimacy with others is a confidence in our own identity."[17] Rachel, in all of her beauty and the love that Jacob bestowed on her, seemed to lack confidence in who she was. Sometimes women find themselves comparing themselves to other women as opposed to capitalizing on all the attributes, gifts, and talents that God has given to them. Stop! Look in the mirror and bathe in the beauty and love that God has deposited into your life. You do not have to envy or be jealous of anyone when you know your true worth in God. Let me remind you

---

[17] Gerald Corey, *Theory and Practice of Counseling and Psychotherapy* 4th Edition (Brooks/Cole Publishing Company, 1991), 110.

through the words of the Psalm 139:14, "I am fearfully and wonderfully made, Your works are wonderful, I know that full well." Essentially, my sister, discover your natural, God-given beauty.

There are men who like big women, and those who like skinny women. And usually both groups end up having someone to love them. But, whether you are a big woman or a skinny woman, you are "fearfully and wonderfully made"; you are victorious. You are a conqueror. Your value and worth should never be given *to* you, but given *by* you.

A Conquering Spirit[18]:

The woman came and knelt before him, "Lord, help me!" she said. He replied, "It is not right to take the children's bread and toss it to their dogs." "Yes, Lord, but even the dogs eat the crumbs that fall from their master's table." Then Jesus answered, "Woman you have great faith! Your request is granted" (Matthew 15:25 ff).

This woman broke all conventional rules and went for what she wanted and needed. She was not swayed, even by discouragement. She held fast to what she wanted from Jesus and would not be stopped. She knew the power of worship coupled with boldness..." She interrupted whatever agenda Jesus might have planned for that day and focused on what she wanted from Him. I submit that when we get to a place where we want a miracle from God, we will push past boundaries, cultural limitations, and racial discrimination. She was indeed a conqueror. She would not be deterred or

---

[18] Kingsley Fletcher, *The Power and Influence of a Woman* (Legacy Publishers International, 2003) 89.

7

discouraged. We need to first decide what it is we want from God. Then, what are you willing to do in order to get it? And lastly, move in the direction of your determination. The world is your oyster! "Whatever determines how you feel on the inside controls in large part the destiny of your life."[19]

You are more than a conqueror! Life at various junctures can bring us face to face with situations that seem more than we can bear. And if we allow ourselves to focus only on the situation, we are already defeated. We need to create a new paradigm of living: "Control, Delete." We must always remember that God is in control, and we need to delete the enemy's power over our circumstances. How do you do that? Allow your daily life to become saturated with the Word. You'll want to have a Scripture quotation for every circumstance in your life. If your back is against the wall, why not Psalm 121: "I will lift my eyes unto the hills from whence my help comes." If you wonder what your future holds, Jeremiah 29:11 (NIV): "For I know the plans I have for you," declares the Lord, "plans to prosper you and not to harm you, plans to give you hope and a future."

If you are perplexed and none of life makes sense, why not: Romans 8:28 (NIV) "And we know that in all things God works for the good of those who love him, who have been called according to his purpose." God has a purpose for your life. Every detail is being worked out. And it is being worked out for your good. God knows your every need. Even though your situation may look bad, and you feel that things will not change; here God reminds you, that He is working it out on your behalf. God knows all there is to know about you and He is in control. You simply need to listen, internalize

---

[19] Howard Thurman, *Deep is the Hunger*, (Friends United Press: Indiana, 1951), 81.

and then actualize. Then it will be easier to 'delete' negativity and live victoriously!

If you want to be a vessel that God will use, it cannot be business as usual. Our desire has to connect with God's desire for our lives. "It's in God's presence that we tap into His life-giving power. Through the shed blood of God's Son, we now have access to God. All it takes is…a sold-out hunger for Him"[20] Pull off every garment that is not like Him. As you change your wardrobe, putting on more of godlikeness, come go with me to the Holy of the Holies!

---

[20] Priscilla Shirer, *He Speaks to Me: Preparing to Hear From God* (Moody Publishers: Chicago, 2006) 149.

CHAPTER 2

The Next Exponential Transformation (NEXT)

As we disrobe the garments that disfigure, disgrace, and distract us from pursuing our purpose, we move to a level in God where we seek more the things that are above; where our affection is wholly to God. If we are to move to that place where we experience God even in the minutia of life, there is a principle and a process.

Principle: In order to obtain all that God has for you, your life has to be saturated by His Word, by prayer and self-denial.

Process: You must follow the steps outlined in this chapter, which takes us into the Holy of the Holies!

Holy of Holies:

Project Runway II: Putting on the Proper Posture to Enter the Holy of Holies

If we are going to enter into the Holy of the Holies, that place of God's dwelling, that place where miracles are a natural occurrence, that place where self is filled with holiness, righteousness, and peace, there is process that must be followed. Our ultimate posture is prostration before our HOLY GOD. I want to touch briefly upon the process and invite you to read more about the Holy Tabernacle in tandem with this chapter. Spend private moments bathing in the knowledge of this sacred and most holy place!

The Gate to the Holy Place

The entry to the holy place was through what was known as the gate. This gate was representative of the entryway to GOD. We as Christians know that the way is through Christ. We have heard about and read the words of Jesus that encourage us and remind us that He is the way, the truth, and the life! (John 14:6). And, He is. If you are searching for truth, you will only find it through Christ. The way to God is through the sacrificial life of Christ. If you are searching for truth, then He is Truth; His word is truth. It is only in Christ that you discover and delight in God. Christ's love is what we need to revel in so that we come face to face with God.

> For God alone my soul waits in silence;
> From Him comes my salvation,
> He only is my rock and my salvation, my fortress;
> I shall never be shaken. (Psalm 62:1–2)

11

Christ is our only way to begin the process of knowing God in a way that is personal and life giving. So, continue to walk with me into the Holy of the Holies.

Christ is the Gate. You must know him. Knowing Jesus is the first insight into what it means to live a life that is set apart from the world, to live a life of self-denial. We have to abandon self in order to be in community with God. We have to silence the voice of the self so that we may perchance hear God. Hearing God calls for intentional listening with the heart. Thank God there is a way to obtain this knowledge. And it calls for more than reading the Word, but also asking the Holy Spirit to help make the Word relevant for your circumstances, to help you hold your life in tandem with what the Word says, and make necessary changes. In silencing the self, it offers a journey into the inner core of being. "Be still and know that I am God" (Psalm 46: 10 NIV).

This process calls for you to center yourself, to bring your wandering mind in to meditate, and consecrate yourself in order to experience the God of your life. Thomas Merton says about this kind of centering:

"At the center of our being is a point of nothingness which is untouched by sin and illusion, a point of pure truth, a point which belongs to God, which is never at our disposal, from which God disposes of our lives, which is inaccessible to the fantasies of our own mind or brutalities of our own will. This little point of ...*absolute poverty* is the pure glory of God in us..."[21]

Emptying self to know self and to know God. Poverty of self is the entryway to the richness of God. At the center of who you are is God. It is a space free of worldly connections

---

[21] Wayne E. Oates, *Nurturing silence In A Noisy Heart* (Augsberg: Minneapolis, 1996), 43.

and worldly desires. Your desire at the core is always for God. I believe that your humanity longs for Divinity. Our finiteness longs for the Infinite. As you continue this process, you are on a discovery of rediscovery. I contend that in the womb, all the intricacies that went into your makeup were saturated with the light of God. As you know, you were created in the image of God. Even though you are stained with the darkness of the sin of Adam, it did not change the core of who you are. The command for you is to return to God. And you can only do that through Jesus the Christ.

By knowing Jesus, we have access to God. Jesus said in John 10:9 (NIV), "I am the gate; whoever enters through me will be saved." Making sure that you have an intimate knowledge of Jesus is the beginning place; it is the first step in the 'process.' Know of His love and His compassion and His Salvation that He freely gives to you. As Jesus wraps His arms around you and all that you are, scars, pain, disappointment, He wants to lead you to that place where nothing else matters but being in the presence of God. It is through Christ that we have fellowship with God. Continue the journey, my sister; the way to God is the way to peace within the self.

Now, as we consider our lives, and what God requires of us to get to a place where His presence dwells, we must continue to deal with the 'self.'

a. *The Brazen Altar*

The Brazen Altar is the place of sacrifice. Your all has to be placed on this altar. Yes, *all* of you. This altar calls for transparency, authenticity, and truth. You bring all of you. Your imperfections, your shortcomings, your needs, your hopes, your attitude, your mistrust, your past pains, your life. Here you remember that Jesus was indeed the perfect sacrifice. He gave his all for you and me. It is the place where you take a closer look at who you really are. You bring to God, the you without makeup, without accessories, without the trappings of the world, just you. If you could simply say, "Naked I came into the world," and then hold that thought, what do you see now? Or whom do you see? This statement should humble you. Because this is how you stand before God. No pretense. No ego to get in the way. No title; just you, the little girl or the grown woman; just you. Not the you who others see you to be. Not the mask that you have been forced to wear to look holy and saved, but who you are, and what is standing between you and your destiny and your purpose.

In the presence of God you become transparent. God sees you as naked. With spots and blemishes and scars of your past and your present, God still loves you. In His presence, you dismount your platform shoes and realize your feet are on sacred ground. You take off the Ruby Woo lipstick and your lips utter pure praise before Him. You remove the make-up of foundations, powders and blushes, eyeliners and lipstick, and the natural beauty of your countenance radiates before God. Natural is the way to God.

In His presence, it is no longer your will but His will; no longer your desire, but His desire. What will you sacrifice for Him? The place to start is your will. Not your will, but *His* will be done. Sacrifice the need to have your way. Sacrifice the appetites of the flesh . . . sacrifice all that prevents God from seeing the reflection of Christ in you. Being in His presence is worth it all! I discover that what stands mostly in my way, is distractions. I have to be careful, or I can become easily distracted. When I know that it is time to read or pray, it seems others things will try to get my attention, such as checking statuses on Facebook or checking messages on the phone. I have to put the phone down, and remind myself to take time to meet with God.

b. The Laver

Now, after removing all the things that can distract, you begin the cleansing process. Before you can approach God, you must be clean. Your heart must be right before Him. You'll recall from biblical history that the priests had to cleanse themselves before they could serve in the Holy Place. The Bible says that we are to sanctify ourselves. Moses was commanded to make a bronze basin. Its sole purpose was for washing/cleansing. (Exodus 30:17). Aaron's sons were commanded to wash their hands and feet before they could enter. (Exodus 30:19).

I work at a hospital, and we are mandated to wash our hands regularly. As a chaplain and the manager of the Clinical Education Department, I constantly remind the students to wash their hands before entering a patient's room, and again on exiting the patient's room. This can easily number 20 times a day. Can you imagine if we would continually "wash" ourselves before God? Cleanse our thoughts, cleanse our ways, and cleanse our attitudes on a regular basis. Then we could move to that place of sacredness and holiness. Christ could see His reflection in us. "By washing their hands and feet, the priests were demonstrating total devotion to God's service."[22] So at this juncture in the temple, there is the laver where one must wash her/himself. We must approach in fear, in awe, in respect, in honoring His mandate to wash, to cleanse

---

[22] Juanita Bynum, *The Threshing Floor* (Charisma House A Strange Company: Florida, 2005) 32

ourselves from every way that prevents us presenting ourselves holy before our holy God. (Exodus 30:17–21, <u>NIV</u>).[23]

c. *The Holy of Holies and the Veil*

The Holy of Holies is the place we should long for. This place is hallowed. It is a place of reverence. Here you will experience the pure presence of God. That alone should cause humility on your part...to be in His PURE presence, not encumbered by the cares of the world, the distractions or barriers that prevent this kind of communion: a Holy Communion indeed! "I with Thou and Thou with me." It's the place where I worship and adore God! In this sacred place, God is there. This is the most holy place in the tabernacle. It is the place all your preparation was leading you to, making you ready for. You cannot come to God unprepared to stand before His holiness. He demands a holy approach to Him! Now, we can come to church any kind of way. We can come in drunk or with a hangover, we can come in as liars, and backbiters, and those with no intentions of living right. The church is that type of place; it is a hospital for the sick. Now, you should not remain sick; there should be something about a song or a sermon that will bring transformation.

People usually go to the hospital to get better, to be cured. So, the church offers all a panacea for every sin sickness. Yes, there is a balm in Gilead. Now, even though the church is a hospital, the holy place is by no means a hospital. The holy place is the place where well folk go, where the redeemed of the Lord enter; yes, where those who have been washed in the blood prepare to enter.

---

[23] (the-tabernacle-place.com/articles/what_is_the.../tabernacle_**laver** assessed July 9, 2014.

During the times of the Levites, they were careful how approached the Ark of the Covenant, for they knew that God would strike them down, if they came in the wrong way. How can you prepare to enter that place? What hinders you now? Do you want more of God? He wants more of you. If you can follow the process to get here, you will experience more of the essence of God, more of His fullness, life, joy, and peace. My sister, you have not experienced the *next exponential transformation* until you have prepared to enter the Holy of the Holies

The Ark of the Covenant

The Holy of the Holies had the most precious, most consecrated piece of religious history: "the Ark of the Covenant and the Mercy seat on top of it" (Exodus 16:3–34). God ordered Moses to place three items: a golden pot of manna, Aaron's staff that had budded, and the two stone tablets where the Ten Commandments were written thereupon. On top of the Ark were two angels, facing each other. They signified God's divine presence and power. What about you? Are you content with the fragrance only, or do you want the perfume of God? Your desire should be: "I want more of HIM."

If you follow this symbolic process and are ushered into God's presence, you can share what is in your heart with Him. He listens. He cares. He answers. You don't have to pretend. God sees that frightened little girl. He sees that insecure woman or that aching heart. Yes, you can bring all of you to Him and bathe in His presence until you experience the kind of liberation where the little girl is no longer frightened, or the woman is no longer insecure and where your aching heart is soothed. But more important than an answer to a prayer is the blessing of being in His holy presence! Wow! To bathe in His presence, to be saturated by His presence is to lose your will in His will...

Now that you are here, you can speak your heart and your heart's desires unto the Lord. Or you can just stand in His presence until you become so intimate with Him that His will is made known and His love for you is expressed and felt within the essence of who you are and all that you will become. It is a place, my sister, where you can communicate your request to Him and He will answer. God already knows the matters of the heart, but He waits for you to share them with Him. He is like a father who longs for his daughter to come and ask for what she desires. And when you leave this holy place you are no longer weighed down by the cares of this world. You begin to realize that in the final analysis, it is only you and God, and that's all that matters. It is that place where you commune with God and God communes with you.

A true story: My husband and I made a reservation to fly to our youngest son's graduation from the University of Michigan. It was cloudy that day, with reports of pending stormy weather and they had cancelled, delayed, and rescheduled the flight. I was told the flight was delayed a few hours so my husband and I went back home to come later to the airport. We headed back to the airport at the rescheduled time and learned that they were canceling the flight. I told my husband we were going to the airport and trust God that we would somehow get a flight. While sitting at the gate, the attendant made an announcement that they were canceling this flight because the pilot experienced difficulty and could not fly into New York. I told her I was going to pray and believe God. I prayed. I asked God to help me to enter at that moment into the Holy of Holies. I knew that if I could get there, my prayers would be answered. I needed God to intervene divinely. There was a young lady sitting next to me who too was desperate to get to her destination. It is amazing how when people believe in God, it does not take much for them to agree in prayer with you. She was a stranger to me but a believer in God and consequently my sister in the kingdom. I was holding Juanita Bynum's book in my hand, *The Threshing Floor*, and I believed everything she wrote about the holy place. Consequently, I was determined to get in position to speak directly to God. This meant I had to prepare myself. I prayed and sanctified myself. I asked for forgiveness of everything that I had done, said, or even thought that was not pleasing to God. I became earnest about what I was seeking God for, and I knew that God would know how serious I was. This moment was so awesome. I experienced the presence of God. There I was, sitting in an airport, surrounded by the noise of other people who were anxiously making decisions to go home, stay in the airport, or go to another gate and try to rebook another plane; I focused on being still and making my journey to the Holy Place. I knew my prayer could not be rote and automatic.

At times, our prayers can become ritualistic. We need to remember that we serve a God of the "now." What is happening in your life now that needs attention? Fresh prayers are called for at times. I am not saying that repeating the same prayer is wrong; I am saying that there are times when we need to take a glimpse at what is happening now and pray a "now" prayer to God.

I urgently sought God in the airport. No, I did not pray out loud and make a spectacle of myself, but I took what Howard Thurman calls the "Inward Journey." I emptied myself of all that would separate me from God. I called on His name. I centered myself. I gave Him honor and praise. I quietly worshiped Him. And before long, I experienced an aweness. I felt a stirring on the inside while I sat in that airport. I was indeed in God's presence. I had just finished reading, and within minutes the same attendant looked at me and said, "Your prayers are answered; the pilot is walking in the door!" Wow, I gave God the praise right then! And yes, we attended our youngest son's graduation!

My sister, you are God's princess! If you can get to the Holy of Holies, breakthroughs are a natural occurrence. Whatever you are seeking God for, He answers! I know some of you may ask, "You tried to enter the Holy of Holies for a graduation?" My response is, yes! God has given you and me the opportunity to come before him. He said that we could come boldly before His throne and ask for what we will. "Let us then approach God's throne of grace with confidence, so that we may receive mercy and find grace to help us in our time of need" (Hebrews 4:16 NIV). As I take my request before him for physical needs, I too go before Him for emotional, mental, and spiritual desires.

Now, allow me to share a story of getting into the presence of God that brought not only my salvation, but also the salvation of my brother. I was in college, and partied most of the time. I was having what I felt was the time of my life. My younger brother experienced a loss of reality. I was floored. He is my favorite brother. We grew up together. When he and my youngest brother were sick, I gave them sugar water and yes, as they told it, they felt better. I was saved when I was a teenager, but I had strayed from God. I had felt the calling of God for me to return to Him. I prayed for my brother. I visited him in a mental institution. My heart was breaking apart. I prayed. And I know that God gave me audience. I sanctified myself so that I would experience God in God's fullness. On a Friday night, I totally surrendered by life to Christ and the next week, my brother walked out of the mental institution. That's a shout right there! That same brother pastors a church, is married with five children, and he has grandchildren that he adores. He and I are still close, talking every morning. He encouraged me to place his story in my book because he felt it had connection to my understanding of how one finds access to God. And he knows the value of going before the presence of God and experiencing transformation, rededication, and holiness.

The saddest thing that a Christian woman can experience is to go through life never having actually experienced God. For many, the closest we get to God is His fragrance. It is like going into a department store and requesting the fragrance instead of the perfume. You cannot feel a fragrance, see a fragrance, or wear a fragrance. There is a process that we must attend to in order to experience the fullness of His presence.

Other Key Ideas from this Women's Retreat:

God's desire for us?

1. To Set us apart: "And do not be conformed to this world, but be you transformed by the Renewing of your mind" (Romans 12: 2 a).

Our way of thinking, acting and living has to be in line with God's Word. It is easy to become distracted by worldly pursuits. God desires us.

He wants to transform our lives so that our desire becomes His desire. Transformation takes place when we determine that it is no more business as usual. God calls us to a higher way of life where breakthroughs and deliverances are a natural way of life!

As women of God, our focus has to change drastically. Many of us have a sharp focus when it comes to the fashion of the world; the latest hairstyles, the right accessories. But I am inviting you to concentrate on the kind of fashion God wants us to wear. The fashion that reflects Him.

2. When we give our lives to Christ, His blood saves us. He died for us and rose from the grave for us so that we might be transformed from the desires of the flesh to the desires of the Spirit, that we might walk in the priesthood toward power. You are the King's daughter, and you should dress like the King's daughter.

The fashion, the clothes that we must take off: bitterness, anger, evil speaking, jealousy, etc. Take it off; it does not fit you anymore. Being the King's daughter, you wear grace, peace, and love. And you wear it well.

We must put on prayer, praise, and worship (there is a difference between praise and worship...praise takes place in the outer courts, worship takes place in the Holy of Holies). Praise is thanking him for what he does and worship is thanking him for who he is.

3. God wants an intimate relationship with us!

Having intimacy with God is the first way to begin producing what is needed to grow in God. Remember, in many places in Scripture we read that so and so "knew" his wife and they begat so and so... I challenge you to see that an intimate relationship with God is the beginning of "knowing" God's desire for you. Knowing God's desire will produce desired outcomes. Each time we take that step toward God, we enter into a sphere of unknown possibilities. I feel safe to say that you want more from God. Well, my dear sister, you and God are in agreement, for He wants more from you. Give Him you.

CHAPTER THREE

Being In the Perpetual Presence of God

Psalm 16:11: "You will make me know the way of life; in Your presence is fullness of joy. At Your right hand are pleasures forevermore."

If He is omnipresence, am I not always in His presence?

The answer is No! It is like being in the presence of air but not allowing the air to come into your lungs. It is like having a nose to breathe but never inhaling and exhaling... Relative to God's presence, unless we breathe in, soak in, bask in His presence, we die spiritually!

In order to come and stay in His perpetual presence, we must deal with the problem of self. As a matter of reality, self is our major barrier to greater blessings and the saturating presence of God. We need to engage in battle with the things in us that prevent us from offering a clean heart before God. After David had sinned and transgressed against God, he cried out in Psalm 51:10, "Create in me a clean heart and renew a right spirit..." God is righteous! To continue in his presence, righteousness has to be our daily focus! We must live our lives in such a way that we pay attention to the smallest detail of transgression. Sometimes it is easy to go from day to day not considering how we treat one another. This is pivotal in our relationship with God. "By this everyone will know that you are my disciples, if you love one another" (John 13:35 NIV).

There was once a staff person in our office who seemed distant and disconnected from the rest of the team. At first I allowed this way of being to continue. I just simply adopted her behavior. I said just enough to be cordial. But the Holy Spirit convicted me. I needed to model God's way! So, I began to speak to her, and I made time to spend moments talking with her. I determined to show kindness to her. If she spoke negatively about a situation, I attempted to get her to see some bright light in the situation. When she complained about others in the office, I began to help her to reframe her thinking and to consider other possibilities for their behavior. For instance, I would say, "Maybe they are struggling with an issue at home and are bringing the residual to work." And then I did something else. I apologized to her for them.

After several weeks of these kinds of conversation, I saw a change in her. I saw a change in me. She became more engaging with others in the office. Her laughter was louder. She smiled more often. I decided to be the change that I was looking for by operating in the framework of what the Holy Spirit dictated for my behavior. What about you? How can you be the change that you want in others? You need to seek opportunities to be an instrument of hope, of change, of transformation for others, as well as for yourself. Being in His presence is to have an unbroken relationship with Him.

Whether you are at work or play, Jesus has to be our ultimate desire. We must not allow our own brokenness to break our relationship with God.

Dealing with Brokenness:

Now and then the question arises, how do I deal with brokenness? Brokenness is painful; it can cause self-doubt, shame, and even resentment. Brokenness can cause you to break away from others. It can bring you to a place of isolation and even mistrust. So, what can you do to begin the process of addressing your brokenness? First you must own the brokenness. Embrace it; for the moment, the brokenness is yours, but it does not have to remain yours. Say, "I am broken but not irreparable. God can fix my brokenness!" We are all broken in some way or have experienced brokenness: broken heart, broken dreams, broken promises, broken relationships. Life has hurt us. We have been hurt by people, and hurt by some of our decisions. All of your brokenness: Give it to GOD! God knows how to turn our brokenness into wholeness, turn our dreams into reality; turn our darkness to light. You may be dealing with brokenness right now in your life, and that brokenness may have you feeling like the whole world is crumbling. Know this: your world is still in God's hand. You remember the song from your childhood: "He has the whole world, in his hands . . . He has you and me sister, in his hands . . . He has the whole world in his hands..."[24] That means he has YOU in his hands, with all your brokenness.

---

[24] http://www.metrolyrics.com/hes-got-the-whole-world-in-his-hands-lyrics-loretta-lynn.html

Allow yourself to feel the fingers of the potter. You remember the Potter! How the potter held the clay that was marred in his hand and instead of discarding it, he made it into a new vessel in which he was pleased. (Jeremiah 18). I believe that some brokenness can be a type of being marred. Life can cause us to experience being or feeling discarded, disregarded: marred. But remember the text's most delicate inference: the vessel became marred "in the Potter's hand." Let's look at the text: "And the vessel that he made of clay was marred in the hand of the potter: so he made it again another vessel, as seemed good to the potter to make it" (Jeremiah 18:4). The vessel, though marred, was still in the hand of the Potter! God holds our messed-up situations in his hands! Now, that is the beauty of serving a God who does not throw us away when we are dealing with our problems, when we are going through our pain. He holds us IN HIS HANDS! That is where your victory is. Even though you may be broken now, you are still in the Potter's hands. Your circumstance, your situation, your painful relationship, your disappointment and discouragement, are all in the Potter's hands!

Moving through brokenness

Let's look at the woman with the issue of blood. History calls her Veronica. Veronica's way through brokenness was incredible. She is our perfect model of how to deal with an issue. When at life's lowest point, Veronica is our girl! She left, on record, a different paradigm for handling brokenness. She demonstrates a path to pursue when life seems over, when hope seems gone.

The Woman with the Issue of Blood (Luke 8:43–48)

Her life was broken by an illness that was present for twelve years. Her daily journey was one of pain and agony. No doubt, she lived a life of isolation. Her shame had her head bowed almost as much as the condition had her body bent. During this long time of brokenness, I am sure she experienced days of sheer loneliness and hopelessness, inferiority and self-doubt. She had to experience alienation from others. She was shunned from public places. She was considered unclean. Can you imagine, not being able to feel compassion? No doubt, Veronica was bereft of affection. The text does not reveal whether she had friends or family, or any support system. There seemed no one available to say, "Girlfriend, you can do it!"

So, Veronica discovered strength within. I believe there is strength within you, even when pain is its companion. There is strength within you though you may be at your lowest point in life. How do I know? "He gives strength to the weary and increases the power of the weak" (Isaiah 40:29). Veronica pushed through the crowd alone. She pushed and she pressed her way. She made up her mind that doctors did not hold her future in their dooming words. She did not allow the lack of money to shape her future. She was broke and broken. She had an issue of blood, not an issue with life! She wanted to live. She wanted the way forward. This woman grabbed hold to what Bishop Paul Morton calls, "a reckless faith!"[25] She resolved to get to Jesus.

The first thing we notice is that she had to discover a way to defeat the crowd. The crowd represents all the

---

[25] Bishop Paul Morton's Sermon: "Dealing With Impossibilities."

barriers in life that seek to prevent you from reaching your transformation and liberation. The crowd is that thing that prevents you from realizing all the power that Jesus has just for you! Power to reshape and to remake you. She was determined to take her brokenness to Jesus. How do you move past the crowd in your life? It may mean that you have to push some people out of your life. It may mean the ending of a bad relationship. Whatever it is that is standing in your way and keeping you from being made whole: push your way through the crowd. Take a page out of Veronica's life. You know what happened when she refused to wallow in her pain and suffering? The issue was resolved in one touch. For Jesus said, "Who touched me?" He told the crowd that virtue had gone out of Him. The blessing that Veronica was seeking, she received. "And he said unto her, Daughter, be of good comfort: thy faith hath made thee whole; go in peace" (Luke 8:48).

In our brokenness, we should seek the virtue of Jesus. We have access to the virtue of our Lord. This virtue is received through faith. Jesus' words to her were, "Your faith has made you whole." Faith was inside of her. Though she was broken, faith was inside of her. Faith did not reside in the doctor. It did not reside in the crowd. It was in her. My sister, your faith is inside of you. You have everything it takes to go to your next level in God. So, with any brokenness in your life, your course of action should be a move toward Jesus. Even though you may not feel like it, or you may be angry now, even with God. You may even feel abandoned by God. Well, you are in good company; remember what Jesus said on the cross, "My God, my God, why has Thou forsaken me?" (Matthew 27:46). Even though Jesus asked the question, he remained in connection with God. He stayed in the perfect will of God. So, feel what you may, but stay connected with God. He has the power over your brokenness. So, move past the crowd of complainers, the crowd of negativity, the crowd of discouragement. Your breakthrough is one touch away!

Stand with your sister who may be broken:

Your sister may experience brokenness, too. Before you judge her *present*, don't forget she has a *past*. Before you judge her *now* remember she had a *then*.

Before you speak ill of her improper way, pause and wonder…and ask yourself, "What happened to her that made her this way?" What you see now in your sister may be the result of what life has done to her. Maybe she did not possess the tools to conquer the negatives that came her way. NOW you meet the consequences of wrong turns, bad turns, even right turns with wrong people, and she no longer looks like the woman that God created her to be. Be a sister to your sister. You can start by listening to her narrative of pain. Hear her story. Listen non-judgmentally. It is true that listening to someone's story has therapeutic value.

I remember counseling a young lady who was in a terrible relationship. Her boyfriend was unfaithful and treated her terribly. She kept trying to hang in there with him and hoped that things would change. They did not. When she came to me, she just wanted someone to listen. She did not need advice or pity, just a listening ear. She was carrying such a burden, and did not trust sharing her story with anyone, but she knew she needed to share it. And so I listened without any interpretation or invitation. She soon garnered the strength to move forward with her life, and the last time I saw her, she seemed happier. She was in a thriving relationship. She refused to accept the blame for his actions. God helped her to reframe how she saw her life and more importantly, how she was able to view her life in a healthy fashion without the abusive boyfriend. Her identity was not connected with whether her relationship with him survived. As women, we need to make room for our sisters. We need to listen to them without giving our opinions and comparing our stories. Allow a sacred space for them to share without fear of being transparent.

Use your Brokenness to minister to your sister

As you are broken, so is your sister. How do you use such brokenness to minister and effect change? Sharing your story is powerful because your sister just might find similar threads, similar themes in her life. Comfort her in the way you wish someone had comforted you. Cry with her, laugh with her, and dance right into the presence of GOD! Be what Henri Nouwen calls the "Wounded Healer" that she needs. It may be allowing yourself to be vulnerable. It may mean taking off your mask of perfection, or your mask of "sainthood." You may have to disclose your weaknesses. Yes, I said it. Too many times we walk around the church looking like we are so together; I mean, the dress is perfect for your size and figure, the designer shoes (fake or authentic) match your designer (fake or authentic) purse. You may look like you just jumped off the cover of *Vogue* magazine, but if the truth is told, your story may be newsworthy for the *National Enquirer*.

Get rid of the pretense and be your sister's keeper. I here invite sisters to begin the process of being open and honest with each other. Pay attention to sisters around you, and check in on your sister. Ask her how she is doing, and then pull up a chair and listen. But listen with the pain of your brokenness, and extend to her what you would need if she were listening to you. Be empathic. Be her sister.

Seek to be in God's perpetual presence. Bring all of you before him and bring your sister along with you. By doing so, you will discover the fullness of life in Christ. David said, "You make known to me the path of life; in your presence there is fullness of joy, at your right hand are pleasures forevermore" (Psalm 16:11). The way of life is not your career, your job, your income, your relationship, or your tangible holdings. The way of life is Christ, our supreme example. The way of life is to be in his perpetual presence. In his presence, you experience joy. Joy is different from happiness; people make you happy, *things* make you happy, and happiness is not permanent, nor can it transcend problems. But joy is grounded in God. And while happiness comes and goes, God places joy within you that helps you to continue to trust in Him. Remember the "joy of the Lord is your strength" (Psalm 28:7). And the twin of joy is pleasure. He promised pleasures forevermore.

CHAPTER 4

Breaking Every Chain

What is it that has you bound? What keeps you up at night? What is it that causes frustration and disappointment? God wants you free! And yes, there is power in the name of Jesus. You can walk into church on any given Sunday and know there are invisible chains throughout the congregation. People may be praising God, but take a closer look at their faces. I hold that we need to pay more attention to each other. Keep your eyes on the finest details because the cliché is true on many levels, "the devil is in the details." It's the seemingly small things that get overlooked. We don't pay enough attention to the nuances of church life. The enemy may have our sister bound and we are so busy noticing her hat that we fail to discover what was on her mind. We are so busy complimenting each other on shoes that we fail to enquire about the other's journey.

The smallest chain must be broken if the Church of the Living God is going to experience a healthy life. It is hard to move freely when you are bound by life's circumstances. Sometimes socio-economic factors can bind one. Prior to an "I'm Just Saying Women's Retreat," I was at a store getting artwork and encountered a lovely lady waiting in line. I initiated a conversation with her and finally asked her to the retreat free of charge. I just felt led to invite her. She came. And later in a conversation with me, she shared that she was so thankful that I had asked her to come.

She stated that she taught school, and the system has stymied her from helping the children gain the educational advantages to move forward in both conceptualization and application. She wanted to give her children an edge so that they could do more than pass tests, not really understanding the subject matter. She felt they wanted teachers to teach kids how to pass tests, and her passion for teaching ran counter to the kind of detachment that was being promoted. The school was short on funding and was apathetic toward the poor children, so she went in her own pocket to try to enhance her instruction. She tried to tap into other resources to make it easier for the children.

She shared with me later that when I invited her to come to the retreat it was an opportunity to take this heavy chain to the Lord. She was thankful for the opportunity to attend the retreat, for the fellowship of other women, and for a sacred place to express her anxiety and frustration. She left the retreat with renewed strength to continue her calling to be there for the children.

If we want God to break chains, it is going to cost us something. It will take prayer and fasting. Prayer cannot be of the drive-by variety. You will need to go before God's face on a daily basis. This intimate relationship must be a priority in your life. God wants to hear from you. And God may not deliver you immediately or break the chain right away. You may have to stay before Him and wait patiently on Him. Patience is a virtue. The Greek word of "perseverance" is *hypomone*, and is also translated as "patience," and "endurance." It literally means to "remain under."[26] In essence, prayer has to be intentionally, intimate and incessant. Reading the book of Job will give you a lesson in Patience 101. When you need God to show up, then *you* show up! Be specific in what you are seeking God for. "Let your requests be known unto God" (Philippians 4:6). If you want God to answer your specific request, then you need to make it specific. God wants to break the chains in your life.

There are some things you are not going to get from God until you fast. Fasting has become a lost power of the church. We fast during Lent, and many go on the Daniel fast (but that is more about losing weight for many). Fasting should have a purpose. If it is indeed a chain that needs to be broken, then lift that problem to God while you are fasting. Though fasting involves the abstention from food, there are those who, for medical reasons, cannot go without food. You can sacrifice something else, i.e. television or your favorite pastime.

Sometimes you can just show up and God will see that you are in bondage and will break the chain then and there. But you must show up. I recall a sermon years ago when Dr. Cesar Clark came to Chattanooga, Tennessee, to preach a revival. Some of the younger ministers wanted to know how he became the giant that he was and how he obtained the status; his answer was so simple: "I showed up." You never know what is going to happen when you show up in the midst of the presence and the power of God. That's what the woman who had an infirmity for 18 years did. Can you imagine if she did not show up that day? What about you?

---

[26] Jeff Doles, *Praying with Fire* (Seffner, FL: Walking Barefoot Ministries, 2004), Kindle Electronic Edition: Chapter 1, 758-60.

You have a chain that you want broken; do you stay home, go to church, or at least go into your prayer closet/room? There are blessings in showing up. She showed up.

Her crippling disease bent her body, and your chains too may bend you in your life. They may bend your hope, your joy, and even your desire to move under the heavy weight of the chains that bind you. Jesus can break every chain. (Luke 13:10–13). The beauty of the text is found in four words, "When Jesus saw her..." Women, Jesus sees you. He knows your pain. He knows your heartache. He knows that which keeps you up at night. And if you trust Him, He will work it out for you.

I invite you to see this woman for the first time. If you look closely enough, you may see yourself. Yes, she is in the church dealing with a chain. She listens to the choir, dealing with a chain; she listens to the sermon, dealing with a chain. And while this may be you, and the sounds of your chains are louder than you can bear, the weight may be unbearable so much that it has bent you into a posture of inferiority, a posture of insecurity, a posture of low self-esteem—Jesus wants to lift that burden. Remember what Jesus said in Luke 4:18: "The Spirit of the Lord is on me, because he has anointed me to proclaim good news to the poor. He has sent me to proclaim freedom for the prisoners and recovery of sight for the blind, to set the oppressed free." Jesus came with a mission, and thank God that mission was clearly for our liberation physically, emotionally, mentally, and spiritually. To obtain this liberation, we must show up, even with our chains. We must show up with the spirit of expectancy. The power of this text is for every woman who has ever experienced a chain and needed the Lord to move on her behalf. "When Jesus saw her, He called her forward and said to her, 'Woman, you are set free from your infirmity.' Then He put His hands on her, and immediately she straightened up and praised God." God wants to set you free.

The Chain of Rejection:

There are women who have dealt with the pain of rejection all of their lives. They may have lived in a home where they were never good enough. Their parents were not nurturers, and they did not experience the warmth of a mother's touch or the strength of a father's hug. They are well acquainted with the pain of detachment. Consequently, they try to win affection in order to feel loved and to feel like someone cares. They seek to live up to others' expectations of them because they want to experience a sense of belonging. "If those who withhold the possibility of being loved have high expectations around our performance in life, then we who feel rejected may go on to try to meet these demanding expectations."[27] Some women live their lives in a vortex of never feeling good enough. This is a chain that Jesus wants to break in your life. Yes, family dynamics and experiences with the withdrawal of affection can have a negative impact on developing a healthy self, but it does not have to define your story. Though someone else may have had a part in writing the first chapters of your story, you can write the conclusion.

At times, this may call for a trip to your therapist's office, to work out the various dynamics that have shaped your present view of self and impacted your existential situation. And while therapy has its place, I hold that the power of God

---

[27] Edward P. Wimberly, *Recalling Our Own Stories,* (San Francisco: Jossey-Bass Publishers, 1997) 17.

yet operates in the lives of those who choose to trust Him. Scripture gives us a clue as to the beauty of our humanity. "I praise You because I am fearfully and wonderfully made; Your works are wonderful, I know that full well" (Psalm 139:14). The question becomes: How do you reclaim yourself? I suggest you discover a way to re-author your own stories. The story that speaks truth about your form and the works that God put into your beauty is very much a part of your story.

My former professor at the ITC (Interdenominational Theological Center), Dr. Wimberly, writes vividly about the various myths (beliefs you have about yourself) that caregivers live with. He helps caregivers see the need to re-author their stories. His masterful way of describing the re-authoring process for the myths in various lives is applicable to the chains that bind us as well:

1. Identify the themes that inform [your] life.
2. Assess whether these themes are producing growth in [yourself and others] or are they contributing to your remaining wounded?
3. Discern the ongoing, continuously unfolding nature of your [purpose].
4. Set goals.

Using Wimberly's suggestions for re-authoring stories may be a good start for dealing with the chain of rejection. If you are presently dealing with some form of rejection in your life and desire to break free from its powerful grip, begin now to identify the themes associated with that rejection, i.e., withdrawal from others, sadness, loneliness, self-doubt, low self-esteem, etc., and reflect on the ways these themes affect your interpersonal relationships. Reflect on the hold they have on you, and your emotional response to others. If these themes are always sabotaging your interactions with others, then continue this process of re-authoring by seeking to discover who God is calling you to be. Once that is confirmed, then set goals to move toward that purpose. God seeks to bring about renewal in your life. God wants you to believe that you are fearfully and wonderfully made. This is not just an ideal you; it is a reality that God wants you to embrace. Rejection has a way of blinding our eyes to the goodness and greatness that God has placed within us.

Gerald Egan, a professor of psychology at Loyola University in Chicago, offers a model of helping that will work well for those who want to move to a place of wholeness; who desire a healthy self-image. Egan's goal is to "Help clients identify, explore, and clarify their problem situations and unused opportunities."[28] Egan introduces us to a process called "Developing a preferred scenario." He helps clients identify what they want in terms of goals and objectives that are based on an understanding of problem situations and opportunities.[29] Essentially, Egan helps clients determine where it is they want to go, recognizing the various challenges and developing an action plan. It may not be easy, but it is possible.

Challenges will come because you are trying to break free from the bondage that causes you to feel unworthy of love and respect. Bondage causes you to live by other people's dictates. You may feel that you need to change who you are in order to earn or deserve someone else's love and admiration.

---

[28] Gerald Egan, *The Skilled Helper*. Fifth Edition, (California: Brooks/Cole Publishing Company, 1994), 23.

[29] Egan, 23.

This bondage is not of God. It is similar to Wimberly's last step in the re-authoring process of setting goals. If you are dealing with rejection, you can begin now to bring about the necessary shift in your life. Your action plan should include a renewal of your understanding about how God sees you. "No, in all these things we are more than conquerors through him who loved us" (Romans 8:37). You can live victoriously, knowing that God loves you and wants you to live a life that is not bound by the chain of rejection. One of the most beautiful passages in the Bible is found in Isaiah 49:16, "Behold, I have engraved you on the palms of my hands; your walls are continually before me." You are ever before God. You are always on God's mind. He will never forsake you or reject you.

Decree and declare who you are in God's sight. Though people who should have shown you love and compassion may have hurt you, you have a choice to re-author your story, to develop a preferred scenario knowing that you are in God's hands, literally. Tasha Cobb said it well; "There is power in the name of Jesus to break every chain."

CHAPTER 5

The Safety Pin

I was ten years old. I was so excited that the fair had come. The fair came to my hometown every year in the month of October. It was special, because October is my birth month. I felt like it was a public birthday party in my honor. On this day, my mom left money for each of us to ride the bus to the fair. Goodings Million Dollar Midway is the name of the famous fair that came to Columbus, Georgia, every year, the second week of October.

On this particular fall afternoon, we rushed to get dressed and ran to catch the bus. My brothers and sister hurriedly ran out of the door and all of a sudden, the buttons on my pants snapped off. I did not have time to find a needle and thread. I began to panic. And then, at ten years old, I cried, "God, please help me!" And right there, I discovered a safety pin on the dresser. I quickly picked it up, fastened my pants, and caught up with my brothers and sisters to catch the bus to the fair. Of course we enjoyed the rides, the cotton candy, the hotdogs, and the Ferris wheel in particular. I loved to ride the Ferris wheel! And I never realized the importance of that day until years later, when I was at a point that I needed faith, and

I needed to trust God and a safety pin appeared! Memories flooded my mind of the October day, as I remembered my anxiety and fear that my brothers and sister would leave me and I would not get the chance to go to the fair. I remembered that in my moment of despair, God was right there.

The safety pin, as small and as insignificant as it may seem, became a point of contact in my faith journey. It became a symbol of trust, a sign of God's presence. Maybe you have never thought about the insignificant things that may indeed have sacred meaning. It may be a place where you find comfort and strength. Life at times may appear to put your hopes on hold, your dreams in limbo. But go within and re-discover your safety pin. Go within and discover those places of new life. Revisit those places that reconnect you to God and others. There is a part of you that is indeed a building block that makes up the construction of your you-ness, as forgotten as it may seem. It may call for you to get in touch with the little girl within you. What glory did you experience in life that you may have forgotten or marked as insignificant? On that fall afternoon, when everyone was running to catch the bus in order to go to the fair for rides, cotton candy and hot dogs, four words made the difference: "God, please help me."

Maybe the buttons on your life seem to be popping off, and you are running out of options. I invite you to go within and tap into the power that God has placed within your reach. Remember the time that you needed God to show up and He showed up. Or remember the last trial or temptation you had and how, somehow, you came through. What was it that gave you the impetus, the encouragement, the wherewithal to move forward? I contend that it is your safety pin. Perhaps you can reconnect some of the disconnected threads of the fabric of your life, to again know the freshness of the move of God in the mundane. May if you reflect on the journey of your life you will see how God has been showing up in ways that, if you were not careful, you would have missed Him.

The Scripture says in Philippians 4:8: "Finally, brothers and sisters, whatever is true, whatever is noble, whatever is right, whatever is pure, whatever is lovely, whatever is admirable—if anything is excellent or praiseworthy—think about such things." There are some things that are pure and noble about you! Reconnect there! Sometimes the ugliness of life has made you think that you are different than what you are. Perhaps the pain has tried to erase the beauty that existed in that little girl with ponytails and bobby socks. Look deeply now...rediscover your beauty, and think on these things. One of the lost things might be your point of faith, your connection to your truth. Many times you may have allowed others to define your reality for you. People get a glimpse at your life and think they know you. Sometimes they refer to you by old labels that were given you. But they don't know you. You are the holder of your stories, as warped and painful as they may be. And since you are the holder, just perhaps, you hold the answers and the resource for change and for re-visioning. If your story is one of pain and shame, may God grant you the power to retell your story through the lens of renewed strength and hope.

The safety pin has been a constant source of connection to the power and presence of God for me. It represents my decision to trust God and to believe against the odds. There are times that I am going through a test, and all indications are that things are not going to change. Without fail, I will pull open a drawer looking for something and a safety pin will be there, reminding me that God is faithful. So think about your own life's journey thus far. What has been that constant, that one thing that kept you true to your faith and your purpose?

The story of Ruth's experience with the extra grains left for her was similar to a safety pin experience. Ruth was struggling alongside her mother-in-law, Naomi. Naomi and Ruth were tied together through a similar loss. They'd both lost their husbands. They could have wallowed in sadness. Naomi decided to go back home. Sometimes home can represent a safety pin. There she could reconnect with the familiar. Ruth wanted to experience not only this familiar, but also the God that Naomi served. Ruth made a decision to follow Naomi back home, declaring that, "Your people shall be my people and your God my God!" (Ruth 2). The story is a love story and a faith story intertwined. The way Ruth recognized that she was well treated was through the extra grain that was left by the reapers. Boaz learned of her loss and how she treated her mother-in-law. When Ruth saw the extra grains, she recognized that Boaz was looking out for her. Maybe this was a type of safety pin for Ruth. (God through Boaz was looking out for Ruth.) God continued to provide for Ruth because as she listened to the wisdom of Naomi, she gained a rapturous love and a husband of significant means.

God looks out for you as well. So as you think about your life, and the many difficulties, wrong turns, and disappointments, what is it that you can name that helps to remind you of the power of God? The safety pin is my reminder, as simple as it is.

Many of us live our lives between the comma and the exclamation points of celebration. That is to say that our lives consist of many pauses and high notes. God gives us a blessing, and we praise and give thanks for the blessing, and then we go back to the pause of going through the motions of life, not actively engaged in doing the work of the Lord. We need God to answer our prayers, and God comes through and gives us what we were expecting. We offer praise and thanksgiving. And then it is back to business as usual; well, at least until we need another miracle from God. For some, this cycle is repeated for the duration of our Christian experience. I suggest here that between the pauses and the exclamation points, we must revisit the safety pin moments, those moments when His presence is near, even though He may not show up in a way you are expecting. He may not appear in the loud noises of life, or in the high praise of a worship experience. He may be in the quietness, the stillness of life.

So, put this book down for a moment and contemplate and identify your safety pin. Once you do that, give God praise for always using that something to keep you together and whole, even between the commas and the exclamation points. Whatever it is, once you discover, or rediscover it, hold it close, for it is God's gift to you to keep you strong even when life does not go according to plan!

A few months before the completion of this book, I was standing outside my church, speaking with one of the ministers. I remember during that day, I was going through my own anxiety about completing this book, and the many obligations that called for my attention. While she and I talked, I looked down on the ground, and there was an opened safety pin. My heart rejoiced, and she rejoiced with me once I shared with her the meaning of that bright, shiny object on the ground. My prayer for you is that you will identify your safety pin and dance like no one is watching!

CHAPTER 6

Defying Labels

Some labels smother the true you. They hide your identity. Can you remember any labels placed upon you? When I was in high school, there was a section of the annual yearbook called superlatives. I now question the title. The reason for my question is that there were such titles/labels as: Most Talkative, Most Flirtatious, Most Friendly, Most Likely to Succeed, and the list went on. These were labels placed on students. And while some of them were true for the moment, they were not true for the duration. Labels are only for a while; they do not define the future. Perhaps you had a label growing up, and it no longer fits you. Labels can be damaging as well as hope-inspiring. For instance, the person labeled Most Likely to Succeed can be motivated to flourish and become the best. Or years later look back at the yearbook and go into a depression because of wrong turns and failure to be good at anything. The friendliest person may yet have the same kind of disposition. But on the other hand, labels like a 'drunk,' 'liar,' or 'drug addict,' and the negative list goes on; these can be detrimental to the ego and to the character, especially if that person has repented and is now redeemed.

Let's consider Martha, the sister of Mary and Lazarus. She has been labeled a worrier, even though we only hear in one place that she was worried about too many things. "Martha, Martha," the Lord answered, "you are worried and upset about many things, but few things are needed—or indeed only one. Mary has chosen what is better, and it will not be taken away from her" (Luke 10:41).

Both sisters were delighted to see Jesus, but as you will see, they expressed their enthusiasm in very different ways. We know that women are different. There are no two of us just alike. We like different things, we enjoy various cultural events; we listen to different genres of music. We like different colors in our clothing, we like different styles of shoes. We like different types of guys; tall, short, handsome, rugged, muscular, slim, stout, chocolate, vanilla, caramel, black cherry, etc. These differences define and separate us, and some of them connect us. Opposites attract. Differences allow our unique character to emerge and soar.

Martha and Mary were different in many ways. Martha was a chef, and it appears that she loved to entertain. Her delight seemed to be in the kitchen, preparing frantically for company and in particular, the often visits of Jesus. I can only imagine the delicacies that came out of her kitchen; delicacies fit for the King. Her desire and intent to prepare a meal to perfection caused her to lose focus during this moment of preparation. I contend that it was one moment, and one moment that did not deserve the label that she sometimes has to wear.

As women we can lose focus when we become too busy with life's activities. Fleeting things distract us. In this day and time, the things that distract us can directly influence our allegiance to God and the things that are spiritual.

For instance, if you are sitting in church on any given Sunday morning, and as the Word goes forth, you pick up your cell phone to check a message or your e-mail, at that moment you lost focus on what God may have been saying expressly to you. As important as messages may be to us, they can wait until church is over. As important as preparing this meal was to Martha, it could have waited until Jesus finished teaching. She had to know Jesus' custom of teaching. I sometimes wonder why she did not prepare the meal *before* Jesus came to her home.

What are the things in your life that you need to prioritize? We all can use more discipline in planning ahead so that we can capture more moments to relax. She, too, could have been sitting at the feet of Jesus. There were no restrictions placed on her such that she was relegated to the kitchen. It is important to note that there is nowhere in Scripture that says this was a habit of Martha's. Martha had the gift of hospitality.

Women bring different gifts into the church. There are gifts of preaching, teaching, praying, singing, leadership, and many more. The gifts that women bring to the church are a blessing to the ministry of the church. One of the sad divisions in the church is that we have some women who are busy doing, and their focus is on getting attention or looking to be recognized or looking for immediate rewards. We as women need to make certain that our reason for being and doing is because of Jesus. We as women need to make sure that we clearly differentiate work in the church from the work *of* the church. Knowing the difference makes all the difference.

It seems that during this visit of Jesus, Martha was labeled a worrier; not by Jesus, but by many who preach this text. Let's free Martha of this label. We have heard Martha the worrier, and Mary the worshipper. I am only referring to this moment. I am so glad that God does not take one moment of our lives and label us. Think about that for a moment. Take a quick moment to survey your past life and reflect on the moments that you are now ashamed of, or moments for which you are so thankful that has God forgiven you. Now tell me, do you want to be labeled by those unsavory moments? I would not.

When I was a college student, I went out one night with friends, and they wanted to spike all of our drinks. I was nearly out of my mind on drugs; I didn't even know what type they were. I went home, and my mother recognized right away that I was not the same. I found a way to lie to her and told her that I did not know who put something in my drink. And of course, she gave me a lecture, but she did it out of love. She did not label me a druggie. It was a one-time thing. I lost focus. I prayed and asked God to help me get through that 16-hour high, and God did. Thank God. I am so glad I was not permanently labeled by that night's incident. And I thank God for the love of a mother.

In our lives, we find ourselves involved in situations that we may regret later. There are some things we wish we could erase from the annals of history. We cannot erase them, but the good news is that our God forgives. And we need to learn how to forgive ourselves. I believe Jesus forgave Martha. He used it as a teaching moment. In essence, Jesus helped Martha to see that she lost focus. She was caught up in *doing*.

The Good Part

Each of us needs to recognize the good part. It was this good part, this priority that Mary placed on listening to the Word that afforded her this high compliment from our Lord. She chose to be with Christ, to listen to Christ. At the moment that Mary sat listening to Christ, she was engaging in the eternal; she was basking in the Word of God. Martha lost her focus on that day. She wanted to serve her guests in the best way that she knew how. Nowhere else in scripture do we hear this label again. As a matter of fact, when we find ourselves at the grave of Lazarus, Martha stands boldly and says, "But I know that even now God will give you whatever you ask" (John 11:22 NIV). This statement seems to have taken Martha from a stage of worry to a stage of faith. We find in John 11:21: "Martha then said to Jesus, 'Lord, if You had been here, my brother would not have died.'" She recognized the power of God in life, but in verse 22 she made a strong proclamation about God's power over death. This does not seem like a worrier, but a person who had learned something about the power of God and spoke it. Later Martha declared in verse 27, "Yes, Lord; I have believed that You are the Christ, the Son of God, *even* He who comes into the world." For Martha to make this statement, somewhere, she chose the "good part" because she could not have made such a statement with conviction if she had not spent some time at the feet of Jesus.

Women, I admonish you to defy labels that are placed upon you. Speak your truth. You are God's child, and your destiny is in you. Momentary slips, or mistakes made in the past do not define you. Every day is a new opportunity to carve out a new you. My sister, with beautiful designer clothes, step onto the runway of your life, adorning yourself in garments that reveal the beauty of God's handiwork. Make God your primary Designer! You are indeed a work in progress; so don't allow others to label you from yesterday when you have moved on to today!

Many of us are guilty of dealing with people on what we've heard about them, on isolated situations in their lives. Maybe you have been the victim of a label. Maybe you are trying to let others know that you are not what you have been called, but your truth is that your life has changed, and you have been empowered. Walk in that truth, not the truth of your past; walk in the truth of today, not the label of yesterday. Continue to believe in yourself and like Lazarus, you will experience dead things coming to life!

CHAPTER 7

Jesus' Compassion in our Tomb-like Situations

¹ They went across the lake to the region of the Gerasenes. ² When Jesus got out of the boat, a man with an impure spirit came from the tombs to meet him. ³ This man lived in the tombs, and no one could bind him anymore, not even with a chain. ⁴ For he had often been chained hand and foot, but he tore the chains apart and broke the irons on his feet. No one was strong enough to subdue him. ⁵ Night and day among the tombs and in the hills he would cry out and cut himself with stones. ⁶ When he saw Jesus from a distance, he ran and fell on his knees in front of him. ⁷ He shouted at the top of his voice, "What do you want with me, Jesus, Son of the Most High God? In God's name don't torture me!" ⁸ For Jesus had said to him, "Come out of this man, you impure spirit!" ⁹ Then Jesus asked him, "What is your name?" "My name is Legion," he replied, "for we are many." ¹⁰ And he begged Jesus again and again not to send them out of the area

[11] A large herd of pigs was feeding on the nearby hillside. [12] The demons begged Jesus, "Send us among the pigs; allow us to go into them." [13] He gave them permission, and the impure spirits came out and went into the pigs. The herd, about two thousand in number, rushed down the steep bank into the lake and were drowned. [14] Those tending the pigs ran off and reported this in the town and countryside, and the people went out to see what had happened [15] When they came to Jesus, they saw the man who had been possessed by the legion of demons, sitting there, dressed and in his right mind; and they were afraid. [16] Those who had seen it told the people what had happened to the demon-possessed man—and told about the pigs as well. [17] Then the people began to plead with Jesus to leave their region. [18] As Jesus was getting into the boat, the man who had been demon-possessed begged to go with him. [19] Jesus did not let him, but said, "Go home to your own people and tell them how much the Lord has done for you, and how he has had mercy on you." [20] So the man went away and began to tell in the Decapolis how much Jesus had done for him. And all the people were amazed.[30]

This text provides an intimate view of the power of Jesus' compassion. It further serves as a model that we should follow as we seek to meet people where they are. There is a darkness that can separate our sisters from the light of God, but it becomes our task to lead her toward that light of hope

---

[30] Mark 5:1–20 (NIV).

and deliverance. As Jesus demonstrated so vividly, we must strive to meet people in their socio-cultural-psychological and emotional-spiritual context. This text produced some tension within me as I wrestled to uncover some of its implications and to recognize what might be the emotional and psychological state of the demoniac. Please park here for a while and wrestle with me so that we can see how strongholds can bind but Jesus can set free.

I determined to look critically at this text and embrace the possibility that the tension of the text might be in the original intent and in a truth that transcends time, culture, or societal constructs. The text called me to make decisions as to how to appropriate a text such as this. "The act of appropriation does not seek to enjoin the original intentions of the author, but rather to expand the conscious horizons of the reader by actualizing the meaning of the text."[31]

The protagonist is a man who became known as the demoniac. This name that has been given to him has ridden the tides of history. It is a name that I feel confident his parents never gave him. And, even though Jesus cast out demons from this man, Jesus never referred to him as the demoniac. It is an insult to the nature of who Jesus is. I believe this because this type of language has unjustly infiltrated the church. I hear the term *demoniac* being used to refer to people who do not act, behave, or respond according to whatever the church determines to be the church's norms. Showing compassion defies categorizing people and relegating them to a name that describes their condition, and not who they are. In this text, mental illness is viewed as being caused by

---

[31] Thompson, 18.

demon possession and as needing to be dispossessed. His mental health forced him out of his familiar environment into a place of seclusion and exclusion. This seems to be the same dynamic that exists within churches when a person's normal way of acting or responding is different because of life changes or life's difficulties.

I wonder what made the graveyard more palatable to him. The text does not indicate whether or not this was a safe place or a sacred place for him to go and experience compassion. When I considered this text from a socio-political perspective, it seemed an act of empowerment and an indirect confrontation to the Roman government and any power that seeks to oppress. In my view of this text from a spiritual view, the healing of this man brought hope and a measure of wholeness. He could thus reenter society, as a witness to the great power of Jesus, and the possibility of rejoining the community in a healthy manner.

The condition of this man could very well reflect some of the pain and suffering narratives within our churches, the lives of all people. Or even you, the reader. This man's story is so familiar that one can hear it from people singing in the choir, shouting praises and sitting in the pews. Their stories reveal their inward struggle to survive, their inner turmoil. Compassion is needed so much. Hurting people simply want someone to listen to their stories of pain and suffering. The stories that we hear in our churches are but a glimpse of persons who feel socially marginalized, emotionally marginalized, and/or financially marginalized.

This man's mental health was at stake. He lived in a tomb. *Tomb* may have a metaphorical meaning. It could very well be a place where the mind goes when life has become unbearable. Could this man's tomb-dwelling posture represent his dissatisfaction with the powers that were surrounding him? Tombs could represent those places where people who are hurting and broken go.

I chose this narrative to be placed in a book written for women because this condition of helplessness and hopelessness is a condition that affects women who come to our churches and work beside us on our jobs. It is further a story of how the power of God, through the person of Jesus the Christ, came to bear on a death-like situation. I reflected on how a tomb-dweller discovered new possibilities and once again returned to his community as a witness. Offering listening opportunities, non-judgmental stances and adequate empathy at whatever location a person is may be the needed panacea. Offering compassion to others has unlimited possibilities!

This man's condition may be a reflection of many people who worship in our churches on a Sunday morning, including those who want to follow Christ and are dealing with emotional and mental problems. Mental illness is a problem within our churches, and many have ignored it and labeled it.

This narrative, which reveals a miracle by Jesus the Christ, may be a didactic moment, a moment that sought to pull at the consciousness of that society and could permeate time. It could indeed have meaning for all of history *and* for our present time. It perhaps has meaning for you and your current situation. It could have relevance for someone you know. It seemed to be an opportunity that Jesus grasped as He noted the power and the injustice of the Roman Empire. There is a plethora of injustices in our times: racism, sexism, capitalism, and the list goes on.

This man who is crying out to Jesus experienced Jesus' recognition of his condition. Into this kind of context, Jesus comes and offers a new paradigm for dealing with mental health, emotional wellbeing, societal structures and abusive powers. "In 5:9 Jesus wrests from this powerful demonic horde its name: Legion. A Latinism, this term had only one meaning in Mark's social world: division of Roman soldiers."[32] How can we work collaboratively to "wrest" from the dominant forces of our society the name of the entity that places unjust burdens on those who are suffering? How can we help those who are struggling emotionally, those who are finding it difficult to manage everyday life? Following Jesus as a model of compassion and empathy, we might attain to wrest again the powers that may prevent a congregant, a sister, or a brother from experiencing freedom and wholeness.

Christians cannot sit idly by and not do the work and ministry that Jesus has modeled and mandated. Even today, we are situated in a society where people are living in tomb-like situations. The church has been empowered and equipped to go and do what Jesus did: liberate!

People are struggling with life's ordeals, and many times because of their response we label them as being mentally ill or we say something like, "She has a demon with that bad attitude," or we may say something like, "That sister is sick," or "Something is wrong with her." Well, if we have made that diagnosis, then as a Christian and a follower of Christ, we need to go to her tomb!!! It's an opportunity to model how Jesus ministered to the man in this text. Let your sister know that you care.

All mental illnesses are not necessarily organic. Sometimes life can deal you a hand that you cannot play. The vicissitudes of life have a way of interfering with what society calls

---

[32] Myers, 191.

normal responses. Many times people respond out of their low reservoir of emotions and are labeled mentally ill.

The text describes this man as engaging in self-destructive behaviors that often serve as an indicator of severe mental and emotional distress or illness. This seems a clear picture of disorganization at best, and disconnection at worst. The diagnosis that the text provides in verse 2 is that he was a "man with an unclean spirit" (*anthropos en pneumatic akatharto*). The word "unclean" in this context typically referred to both ritual or ceremonial and moral uncleanliness. Later in the story, the author will identify the man explicitly as *daimonizomai* or "demoniac." The fact that it was an alien spirit that was in or with this man is emphasized by the fact that Jesus eventually expels the spirit by performing an exorcism, thereby releasing the man from its possession. This allows the man to resume his identity and character, which the text describes as *sophroneo*, which means to be sober, under control, or of sound mind.

But if one stops there, then a grave injustice occurs. Other dimensions are seeking our attention. This story emphatically invites the modern-day reader into the heart of hearts, of Jesus' response to someone who is hurting and discovering the difficulty of managing daily activities. We are not privileged as to the intimate details of this man's life, his family's dynamics, or the when and where of his ability to provide for himself or a family. But glaring through the shadows of this text is a living human document[33] whose life had apparently come crashing down and who needed what Jesus had to offer. And perchance some woman whose life is falling apart right now needs you to help her re-vision

---

[33] Dykstra, *Images of Pastoral Care: Classic Readings.*

and reframe her story. Through a powerful dialogue, he was offered the opportunity of re-entry to a life of wholeness. What dialogue can you have with your sister to begin the process of her healing?

Jesus' approach to the condition of this man is the paradigm that we need to honor and use in our response to those we encounter at the crossroads of life; that place where life seems to run counter to what seems normal and disables one from functioning effectively. This passage of Scripture gives me a biblical response to mental health. Women are suffering from bad relationships, failed marriages, failed careers, and their very lives have crashed upon them. They are crying out for help. It seemed a beckoning call to the church, to you the reader in particular.

Consider some of the things that Jesus would deconstruct relative to the operation and non-operation of the church. The church must look in the mirror and change some of her ways. When people come to our churches in the clutches of mental health crises, perhaps our duty is to approach them with a compassion that Jesus had for the man who was known as the demoniac. We cannot simply stand by and sprinkle oil and call it a quick fix. As Jesus took time to go to the other side, we too must follow Him. We must provide a sacred space for people to share their pain and perchance recover their souls.

A story to ponder: recognizing mental distress in your circles

How aware are you of those around you? We are our sisters' keepers. We need to pay more attention to each other. We sit together in the church pews. We attend some of the same meetings. We eat at some of the same restaurants. We may even be sorority sisters. When was the last time you asked your sister, "How are you doing?" and then pulled up a chair. I once invited a social worker to come to my local church to help others be aware of possible mental health issues within our congregation. She shared with me in an earlier conversation about some of the issues that she dealt with on a daily basis. I felt that she could frame her workshop in such a way that it would address some possible issues within the church. My goal was to help make us more sensitive to each other. I wanted to increase the awareness of mental distress that occurs in the midst of all the praise and worship on any given Sunday.

Before the social worker's scheduled presentation, I read a story in the news about a young woman who drowned herself and her children in the Hudson River. I wrote a poem about it and used it in the devotion during the first seminar.

> *You saw my pain but never asked me any questions, you saw my tears but never asked me why do I cry. I sat next to you at church, but you never asked about my day, you continued going along your merry way, There was pain in my heart, and trouble I did not know how to share, I was not sure if you would even care. So, when I could take no more I made personal plans to end it all. And now you wonder, some of you call me crazy and say all kinds of mean things about me. But you never asked me about my story, and now you sit and quiver, because I took my children and we ended in the Hudson River!*

The poem referenced how she may have publicly showed her pain, but how those around her did not notice the signs of her mental distress. The social worker then began her seminar with the article about the above story.[34] There were loud "Amen" and "Lord help us" from the audience. I had asked her to speak about that story since it had been in the news, and it had stirred people in the community. She shared the importance of people in the church being more attentive to those who sit in the same pews with them every Sunday.

The social worker had put an article in her packet that defined the various disorders.[35] She engaged the attendees around their responses to mental health issues and what God commands of us as we seek to love one another. She shared that the church should want to address various issues in whatever medium is necessary in order for God's love to be incarnate in each of us.

Sisters, let's begin to see more than what types of shoes our sisters are wearing and what latest style she may have on. Let's see more than what ministry she serves in the church, and how loud she may praise our God. Let's see her! It is easy to look happy when you are around other people in our churches who are looking happy, or in fact they are *trying* to look happy. We will never know what is going on with our sister until we began to show her true hospitality.[36] The next time you ask your sister how she is doing and she says to you, "I am doing OK," ask her to define "OK" and listen carefully, because her response may offer you a clue as to

---

[34] Daniel Bates and Mark Duell, www.dailymail.co.uk/LaShanda-Armstrong-drives.(Accessed 21 April 2011).

[35] http://www.webmd.com/mental-health-types-illness?print=true. (Accessed 20 May 2011).

[36] Henri Nouwen

what is going on in her inner world. It may bring you closer to the tomb where she dwells, to the chains and fetters that have bound her. You may help to dry her tears and even stop the emotional cuts that have become a part of her daily life.

Perhaps you can determine each day to check on at least one sister in your congregation, in your workplace, or your community. Simply ask, "How are you?" and then pull up a chair and listen. Listening is therapeutic. You may be surprised at the healing moment that occurs. You may liberate a sister from the tomb of her mental anguish. You may indeed partner with Jesus as you, too, dare to go to the tomb-like situations of your sister who is sitting on your same pew, or two pews down. Look for her; she is there. Can you see her?

CHAPTER 8

Moving Toward Your Purpose

Being a clinical pastoral educator has allowed me the privilege to walk the journey with many students, to dialogue with colleagues who train in both clinical supervision and who run private practices. The cross-pollination has increased my understanding of people's needs. What I have learned, and what matters most to me, is the value of listening. We need to provide an avenue where people feel heard. I need to offer a caveat here: sometimes you may be on your own. Or feel like you are. There may be no one to listen. During these times, it is my prayer that you find the strength and the wherewithal to encourage yourself.

While you may want someone to listen, there comes a time when you must tap into the power within you. Within each of us lies a survival mechanism called purpose. Oh yes, you have one. Seek it until you find it; once you do, there's no stopping you!

Viktor Frankl shares his story[37] when he was in a prison in Auschwitz. In the midst of all the torment and torture, he

---

[37] Frankl, Viktor. *Man's Search for Meaning (Peo4th Edition) {Revised & Updated}*, Boston: Beacon, 2002.

came to a conclusion that those who endure suffering have to consider and hopefully embrace. He had to go within himself to discover the wherewithal to survive. He makes it clear that if he had focused on what life had brought across his path it would have hindered him from surviving. Frankl ultimately demonstrated how one should live life with a purpose regardless of pain, disappointment, and suffering. There is so much strength within us that goes untapped.[38] It was through my encounter with his book that I discovered ways to help women utilize the power within, even when life does not seem fair. It allowed me to reflect on the value that I place on things in life. "Things" are wonderful, but having and knowing your purpose is the greatest blessing. It will drive you, motivate you, sustain you, and keep you when life seems unbearable.

There are times that we have no control over external events in our lives. Frankl maintains that we do have control over how we respond to those circumstances. As we come to recognize that we have a purpose, that purpose will take the driver's seat in our lives. Even though we may pass through bumps in the road, and sharp turns and sometimes a head-on collision, our purpose keeps our hands on the steering wheel of our lives. If you are to survive this life, your highest purpose has to be discovered. This can only be done by spending time with God. I am convinced that if we can learn the art of silence, we will hear the voice of God's directions for our lives. "For God alone my soul waits in silence; from him comes my salvation. He alone is my rock and my salvation, my fortress; I shall not be greatly shaken" (Psalm 61:1–2 ESV). Life's circumstances can fill

---

[38] Ibid.

our lives with perpetual noise. "Your life may be a battle of contending forces. The rattle and noise of battle weighs your heart down."[39] Wayne Oates teaches us to nurture silence; we have to determine to find that time alone with God. It is those intimate moments that God speaks directly to us, defining our purpose.

Our stories have a direct impact on our destiny. We are the authors of our stories. And as the author, we can write, erase, and rewrite every line afresh. We cannot allow others to define us and tell us how our stories should start or end. Our stories belong to us. The grace of God helps us to shape our stories so that they reflect more of Christ and less of us.

Your birth was not an accident. You belong. You are needed. No one else can live out the purpose God has deposited deep within you. You may have to spend some time in silence in order to "discover afresh the Center of you that is not you—it is God."[40] God calls us back to Himself so that we might attain all that He has for us.

While you determine to claim your power and your purpose, you will soon recognize that there is more power within you than there is outside of you. Scripture says explicitly to you and to me, "But you belong to God, my dear children. You have already won a victory over those people, because the Spirit who lives in you is greater than the spirit who lives in the world" (I John 4:4 NLT). This alone should elevate you to a new level of thinking. Frankl tapped into the power within. When you read his story, you'll learn that he had to live through the ordeal of death all around him, and he chose life. When you read his story, there was nothing

---

[39] Wayne E. Oates, *Nurturing Silence in a Noisy Heart* (Minneapolis: Augsburg Fortress, 1996) 35.

[40] Oates, 90.

good going on without. His whole world was a gamble on whether he would live or die, whether he would survive the onslaught of hate and evil. And he did! It did not come easy; he first had to change his mind-set.

Frankl made his inner perspective greater than his outer reality. Within him was a strength that his circumstances could not diminish. You can garner the same strength. And if you feel that you are too weak right now, ask God to lead you to someone who can walk this journey with you; someone who has weathered the storm before. And if you have survived severe tests and trials, share your story with other sisters so that they, too, might gain encouragement to fight against all the odds and move to a place called hope.

"In our own time, such thinkers as Bruno Bettelheim and Claude Levi-Strauss have argued that stories provide us with an emotional catharsis which in turn leads to personal integration."[41] As we recognize that our stories, whether negative or positive have meaning for our lives, we will want to share them. Our stories, if told through the lens of hope and possibility, will not only be therapeutic for us but for countless others who may be struggling with life's problems and are in need of strength and encouragement to move on and toward their God-ordained purpose. There are positive elements within our stories that may serve as an impetus for imbuing self-worth and dignity, even in your present reality.

"Since we live so much of our self-identifying narrative unconsciously, the caregiver's first task is to make the unconscious conscious."[42] As a counselor, and as a caregiver, it becomes my duty to walk the journey toward revelation

---

[41] Philip Culbertson, *Caring for God's People: Counseling and Christian Wholeness* (Minneapolis: Fortress Press, 2000) 44.

[42] Ibid. 45.

and interpretation of the issues that are stated during an encounter. Underneath many stories are repressed memories. These memories may be crucial to moving toward healing and wholeness.

We must embrace all of our stories in order to discover our true identity. When I was a little girl, my mom often told me stories about my life of which I was not aware. For instance, she shared that when she was pregnant with me, she had a difficult time, and the only thing that brought her and me through the pregnancy was prayer. She further shared that two weeks after my birth, she and my dad had to take me back to the hospital and while in the hospital, I stopped breathing and started to turn blue. My father opened the incubator and began to pray for me, and my breathing and color returned. When my father preached revivals, he would call me up to the front seat and share with the congregation that I was his miracle child. He expressed it as a miracle through the power of prayer. This part of my story has so much meaning that God moved me from a difficult gestation period to my struggle to breathe until my father prayed for life for me. Prayer is a strong force in my life. Over every situation, I believe prayer is in order. Pray in the good times, a prayer of thanksgiving, and pray in the bad times, a prayer of petition. Prayer is always in order.

People share their problems with me and after listening and processing their issues, I privately take their situations to God in hope for new life. New life is always possible. One way to stay connected to others is to pray with and for them. Call their names. Don't you know of someone now who needs prayer? Call their names now! Seek God's blessings for them. You just might save a life or change a situation.

What's your story? What are the themes that shape who you are? If you have not already, revisit the lines of your story with all the good, the bad, and the ugly, and then own it! It is yours. I remember at one of my retreats, the women were asked to participate in a session called: "It's Your Story, Let Me Tell It." The reason I added this session in the retreat is because many women are dealing with shame issues and problems that they don't feel safe sharing. I knew that in this session, they could write their story/ies honestly on an index card and drop it in the basket anonymously. No one would know the identity of the owner of the story. This proved to be a blessing, and my facilitators and I began to address the issues by sharing our responses in a non-judgmental and compassion-filled manner. All of my facilitators are trained clinicians; one is a social worker, and the other three are trained in clinical pastoral education; two of whom are board-certified chaplains and board-certified pastoral counselors. The stories were many and varied. Stories of abuse and pain and suffering were released to receive the blessings that God had foreordained. Many women came afterward and identified themselves, stating that the session was healing and life-giving for them.

Sometimes remembering our stories can bring pain and loneliness. At times it may require counseling, but it is possible to move to a place where you can draw from the well of understanding self, from self-forgiveness and forgiving the one who caused the pain. Unforgiveness holds us captive. My father (who is now deceased) traveled every week doing revivals or attending to preaching engagements. I cannot remember my father ever going to a school play, watching me as a cheerleader or even asking about my homework. For years I held bitterness in my heart against my father. Even though, I said kind things about him, there was a pain that would not go away. It was while I preached about forgiveness that I was convicted to let it go. Yes, the pain is there when I remember it, but the bitterness no longer holds me captive because I forgave him. I did it for me.

There are stories that pain us, and I pray that God will allow you to discover new paths to your spiritual and emotional health. I hope you will come to a place where God will give you the ability to re-author your own story. Hopefully you will discover that your story has an impact on your destiny. My prayer is that you will learn to use the negative as a resource to minister to others, and the positive as wind beneath your wings as you soar to the height that God has purposed for you.

CHAPTER 9

To Midwife My Sister

The power of true sisterhood is to give birth to moments of liberation. It is the offering to walk the journey during the other's travail, the other's labor pain. "One of the first things a midwife must learn is *what travail looks like!*"[43] Many of our sisters and sometimes we, too, have faced travail on many levels. We do not shrink from it but attend to it. "In order to be a good spiritual midwife...it is necessary to have experienced rebirth, to have passed through some sort of spiritual travail oneself."[44] Our experiences help us to help each other....

As midwives, our calling is to assist "God in birthing new life in people and in their relationships with self, others, the world, and God."[45] We listen to their stories, help them first to discover their spiritual resources, and then empower them to utilize those resources. This in itself is a birthing process. As sisters who midwife one another, we have embraced the blessedness of our ultimate purpose: to help bring about new

---

[43] Ibid. 206.
[44] Ibid.
[45] Ibid. 207.

life, new hope, or at least a new lens through which to view pain and suffering.

Ministering to people who are at various stations in life, and some who are swinging on the pendulum between life and death, requires that we pay attention to one another. There is a place of intimacy and transparency, of knowing and being known in providing care. For the most part, people I have encountered are either searching for some form of intimacy that transcends their particular illness, quandaries about life, suffering, sickness and death, or they simply want someone to listen to whatever their ponderings are at whatever stage of life they may be in. People wrestle with different issues in life, including death and dying and all of its dark secrets. There are many coping mechanisms, but none comes close to having sisters who are willing to midwife one another. There is strength within each of us to forge forward, regardless of our circumstances. At times we need the gentle touch and company of our sisters who will stand with us between reason and doubt, between fear and faith, and help us give birth to new opportunities. This same reflection has helped me to be attuned to the possibilities of empowering others in their dilemmas, be it any level of suffering. All of us have faced difficulties that involved some area of suffering, and we are well aware of the things we wished had been in place to begin healing. Having self as a resource is beneficial. People are facing difficulties each day, and some of these difficulties are coupled with destructive forces. Forces such as discouragement, disempowerment and a lack of willpower can negatively affect people's lives. Creating that safe space to share these dynamics and emotions can be a "balm in Gilead."

"To heal the disconnections that divide us we must look at what Volf calls 'powerful, contagious and destructive evil of exclusion'." (1996, 30).[46] By navigating such divides with compassion and conviction, God calls us to be with people during their moments of hoping against hope.

Accepting people as they are is the order of the day (unconditional positive regard).[47] It seems that too many times, church folk want to fix people, and not listen to their stories of pain and frustration. God's design for us is to live healthy lives physically, mentally, emotionally, and spiritually.

When I was in seminary at the ITC (Morehouse School of Religion) in Atlanta, Georgia, I went through a terrible relationship problem; I did not have words to express what was happening inside me. My best girlfriend, Chaplain Lieutenant Colonel Grace Hollis, the resident's assistant of Turner Hall, the dorm where I lived, said to me, "You are hurt, just let me scream for you!" She screamed for me. That scream was cathartic for that moment, but left me with a question, "Why couldn't I scream for myself?" I knew the answer; I had an image that I was trying to protect. I had resigned myself to wearing a mask that was shared by the Pentecostalism of my parents. "In all things trust Him; to doubt is to sin." I trusted then and now, but I know that sometimes screaming gives release. It does not mean that I trust God any less. There are those times in our lives when we feel that God is nowhere around, as if we have to go it alone.

In the church where I grew up, screaming was not allowed. You prayed everything out. Though I left the church and came back, I fell back into the prescribed way of responding to problems. This caused me to stuff my emotions in an effort

---

[46] Sheryl A. Kujawa-Holbrook and Karen B. Montagno, Editors, *Injustice and the Care of Souls* (Minneapolis: Fortress Press, 2009), 31.

[47] Rogers, Carl, *On Becoming a Person* (New York: Constable and Robinson), 1977.

to appear holy. I did not have the courage to be, particularly within the sacred walls of the church.

But I have learned the importance of helping people journey toward "self- affirmation…"[48] I so desire to help people, and my sisters in particular to feel at home, because at home we feel safe and free to utter our despair. At home many of us even sing in the shower, and we would not dare attempt to sing the slightest tune in the church. But at home we feel comfortable to be. I propose that a woman should feel free to be at every juncture in her life, at every step of her journey. It is that kind of liberation we should want to give to each other. We should midwife each other toward giving birth to a free self. In order to be a good midwife, "It is necessary to have experienced rebirth, to have passed through some sort of spiritual travail oneself.[49] For you cannot recognize travail or a journey toward spiritual renewal if you have not gone through that process.

"Our calling necessitates that we are person-centered. We are in the business of assisting God in birthing new life in people and in their relationship with self, others, the world, and God."[50] We must see our sister as a unique person with a life of her own; a career, a family, likes and dislikes. Her personality is different from yours and the next woman in the room. When we attempt to assist her, we must see her in all of her uniqueness. We cannot compare her to any other woman because she is her own woman. Life has shaped her into the person that she is, and she may experience labor pains

---

[48] Paul Tillich, *The Courage to Be,* 2nd Edition, (The Terry Lectures), (New Haven: Yale University Press, 2000), Kindle Edition, location 200-204.

[49] Ibid. 207.

[50] Dykstra, 206.

entirely differently. To midwife calls for you to pay attention to the nuances that make her who she is. Be there for your sister. Your role is to help her move through the travail, to comfort her during the pains of birth. It is not the job of the midwife to determine the outcome.

CHAPTER 10

From Pain To Power

I was privileged to hear the story below. I felt honored that it was given to me to write anonymously to encourage other women who have gone through a painful past that seeks to bind them and rob them of a glorious future.

"I was 12 years old when I lost my innocence, and it was not by my consent. I didn't know much about 'the birds and the bees' except the few things my mother taught me. Back during that time, we received sex education classes in school; however, it was limited to classes that discussed the changes girls and boys underwent when they reached puberty. In retrospect, nothing would have prepared me for what I was about to experience, or the lasting effects that one night would have on me in the years to come. I have never recalled the actual date of the incident, or the year for that matter, until I was asked to put it into words. I only remembered my age.

"Forty-five years ago, on a Saturday night, May 10, 1969, I decided to get my things prepared for church, for the next day was Sunday, Mother's Day. I guess I finished watching television around 10:30 p.m. or 11:00 p.m. and turned it off.

Although there was a television in my parents' room, we did not have televisions in any of the children's rooms. The main television was in the living room.

"I wanted everything to be perfect for my mother on Mother's Day. I was determined not to cause her to wait for me to get dressed and make us late for the worship service. I ironed my clothes and laid them out so it wouldn't take long for me to get dressed. I laid out the usual items; shoes, socks, underclothes and a dress. I guess by this time, it was a little after midnight, so I went to take my bath and wash my hair. I thought if I got everything done that night, the entire family, mother, father, two-year-old sister and 11-year-old brother, would not have to compete for the one bathroom in the house Sunday morning.

"We lived in a two-flat apartment building, and my mother and father owned the building. There was a three-bedroom unit upstairs, and we lived on the first floor. In our house, there were stairs that led to the basement, which was additional recreational space when we had company to entertain. In the actual house, my parents' room was in the front of the building next to the living room; the bedroom that I shared with my two-year-old sister was down the hall from my parents' room, and on the opposite side of the hallway. The one bathroom that we all shared was down the hall, and on the opposite side of the hall from my bedroom, but adjacent to my parents' room; and if you kept going you would encounter the kitchen, which had a back door, and it was adjacent to the bathroom. Around the back of the house, opposite the kitchen, was my brother's room, all tucked away and right off the kitchen pantry.

"In the front of the building there were stairs from the ground level that led to the front door. There was also a window, right off the living room that protruded onto the front porch. We never thought that someone would illegally access our home from the front porch, and come through the living room window. Who would have thought someone would do that? Years of living there and never a problem. Ever!

"I was hoping that my hair would be dry in the morning so that I would be able to comb it out quickly and go. I didn't have a perm at that age, and I didn't know anything about a blow dryer. When I finished bathing, washing, and braiding my hair, I donned my nightclothes and turned off all the lights in the house. We had ceiling lights that had the pull chains in the bedrooms; there were lamps in the living room, and wall switches for both the kitchen and bathroom. Everyone else had already retired to bed several hours before. I was the only one stirring in the house; but now it was time for me to go to sleep. It was about 1:00 a.m. or so, I don't remember the actual time. All refreshed, I fell sound asleep!

"I was awakened suddenly. Now, I was disoriented! It felt as if someone had fallen on top of my back. But why? I am a stomach sleeper; even until this day I still sleep on my stomach. I struggled! A man's voice said, "Be quiet." His hand was covering my mouth and nose. The only thing I could do was lay there. I was trying to figure out who this person was on top of me. I thought it was my father, but it was not his voice.

"The smell of this man, and his breath was utterly nauseating. How did I get on my back? Somehow, he made me roll over onto my back. He proceeded to kiss me all over my face and nose. It was nasty, wet, and disgusting! The smell of him and his breath was really unbearable for me, as I had never smelled anything like it before. I was trying not to breathe. However, I couldn't hold my breath for long. What was he trying to do? Was that a metal object on my neck? What the heck is going? on I thought. Why is he here and in my bed? His body was between my legs. He was going to have sex with me. He was trying to penetrate me. I told him he was not going to fit; he was unable to get it fully in.

"I reached out my arm in order to wake my two-year-old sister up. How could she sleep? I thought to myself. I kept shaking her while he was still on top of me trying to fully penetrate me. Finally, she calmly woke up, as she didn't know what was going on. She was too young and only two years old. All I could think about was getting out of that room. So, I told him my sister needed to go to the bathroom, and I didn't want to lay there in pee. He agreed that I could take her to the bathroom. But he got up to escort us.

"The room was pitch-black. I began reaching for the pull chain to the light in the center of the room. Where is that pull chain? I thought. Any other time, I would have no problem locating that darn chain; but I couldn't find it this time. I wanted to see the perpetrator's face; the person that had the audacity to break into our house and do this to me. Who was it? It was apparent that he had been watching our house, waiting for his chance to break into the front window.

"Where is Fluffy? He was a beautiful tan cocker spaniel, maybe not even a year old. Why didn't Fluffy bark? Did our dog know this person? Or, is this a breed that just doesn't bark? Probably! Anyway, he proved to be no watch dog. Useless at least for that purpose! In retrospect, it was probably a good thing that I did not find that pull-chain and turn the light on. Who knows what harm could have come to my sister or me.

"I held my sister's hand with my right hand and he held my left hand in order to escort us to the bathroom. I proceeded to cross the threshold to my bedroom. I went to my right. It was in the direction of my parents' room. He said, "The bathroom isn't that way!" How does he know this? I thought to myself. Suddenly, I fell to the floor with my sister in hand. I screamed loudly! He ran in the direction of the kitchen. Apparently, he had already opened the back door, I suppose for a fast getaway. With all this commotion going on, now my father was awake. He grabbed his gun and gave chase after the man. He fired several shots and missed him. I was saddened that he didn't shoot him. It was pitch-black outside, and the perpetrator had a head-start escaping from the house.

"By this time, my mother had phoned the police. When they arrived to the house, they told my mother that I had to go to the hospital in order to get checked out by a doctor. I really didn't want to go. So, I was sitting in the emergency department; now it was about 4:00 a.m. A doctor entered the treatment room. Now, I became scared. I was expecting a doctor to look like Dr. Ben Casey or Dr. Kildare on television. These were the only other doctors I could reference outside of my pediatricians. The doctor wore a blue wrinkled top and matching bottom (scrubs). He didn't look neat; therefore, he did not look like a real doctor to me.

"Then, the nurse entered the room. I felt much better now. She was dressed in all white and had on a nurse's cap. She walked over to the exam table I was sitting on and asked me to put my legs up in the stirrups. I reluctantly complied. Now what the heck is he doing down there! I looked over at my mother and saw that she was in tears. My father chose to stay home. His only concern was that, if I was a virgin, why didn't I bleed. Well, I don't know why I didn't bleed. But, I was a virgin!

"The doctor inserted a cold metal thing (speculum) into my vagina. Again, what is he doing? He asked me if I was a virgin, and I replied in the affirmative. Then he asked me if the man ejaculated in me. What? What is that? Well, I guess he answered his own question. He told us there was no sperm in my vagina, and he was unable to take a specimen for forensics. Yuck! The nurse walked over and said she needed to give me a shot that would help prevent venereal diseases. I was only 12 years old; I didn't have a clue as to all these questions or what they were saying to me.

"After the visit to the emergency room, the police drove my mother and me home. I don't remember if my sister was with us. I exited the police car and began walking toward the front stairs. Everything was as if it was in slow motion. I walked up the front stairs. I glanced over at the living room window where the unknown man had broken and entered our house. I entered the front door of the house. Then it hit me! The smell! It was awful, and I didn't want to stay in the house. The house still smelled like that unknown man who had broken into the house. He was inebriated, and he had our house reeking of stale alcohol. I could still smell it two hours later. That was an unbearable moment for me too! I couldn't bear the smell of the house. I do not even think my mother was aware of what was going on in my head. I entered the house and went to my bedroom. I reluctantly opened the window; I had to air out the room.

"Needless to say, we didn't go to church that Mother's Day. My mother and I never talked about the incident. Unfortunately, there is an everlasting imprint of the events that transpired in my life for that moment in time. The fact that we never knew the identity of the perpetrator caused me to think that every man I encountered on the street thereafter, or that stared at me longer than three seconds, was he.

"I thank God Almighty that neither my sister nor I was killed. It was his grace and mercy that saw us through that ordeal. That perpetrator could have escaped from the kitchen door after causing serious harm to my sister and me. Thank God I remained calm in the midst of my enemy and had the *wherewithal* to get out of that room by mandating to take my sister to the bathroom. Unfortunately, there were two other rapes that took place that year in the neighborhood.

"The old adage, "What doesn't kill you, makes you stronger," is true. However, the question is, "At what cost?" How traumatized do I remain, even 45 years later? Do I still replay this event in my mind's eye? How long did it take before I stopped believing that every man I encountered was the perpetrator that broke into our house that Saturday evening? It was and is a process of believing that I am fearfully and wonderfully made, and though I remember graphically this intrusion upon my innocence, I remember the mercy of God that night. I remember the wisdom God gave me to ask to take my sister to the bathroom. I remember the wherewithal to scream loudly until help and deliverance came. I see God's mercy over my and my sister's life. This incident could have prevented me from moving forward; it could have caused me to lose my mind. But through the grace of God I stand firm, and I moved into my purpose. God blessed me to finish college and grad school and gave me a successful career. Perhaps, you may say, I should have gone to therapy; but treatment was not popular during that time. I had to rely upon the God of my Sunday school classes. I relied on the God that I was introduced to by my mother. And I discovered it to be true that God does journey with us through our pain, through our questions, through our darkness, and He does give light. I had to lean on God.

"I was determined that the unknown man would not rape me of my destiny. I refused to wallow in the blame of my father's cold words and the inability of my mother to talk to me about it. Maybe her pain was too intense; maybe she felt she failed me. Maybe she did not have words. I forgive her.

"I had to forgive my father for his insensitivity. When I needed him most after being violated, he was not there for me. I thank God that my Father in heaven stood with that little girl, and he stands with me today.

"The images of that night are still vivid in my mind, but they do not control me. The sadness of that night is palpable, but it does not have power over my ability to move toward my destiny. To this day, I still cannot stand the smell of alcohol on anyone's breath. I do not like to be kissed all over my face. In fact, I hate wet kisses! I do not like being startled while I'm sleeping. In general, I am a light sleeper. It took decades before I could get the nerve to live alone in a single-family dwelling. But now, I have moved from pain to the power of being. I refuse to let that dark night rob me of my bright future. I refuse to be stuck in my past when my future is so promising.

"Forty-five years later, I struggle with the evils that caused that night to happen, but I struggle in God and with God and through the presence of God! So, whomever you are, you did not break me! Praise God! Yes, it was a painful, heartbreaking moment in my life, but God moved me from pain to power! Power to live, power to move forward, power to say yes to life! So, women, whatever pain may have come your way as a child, as a teenager, even as an adult, don't let that pain destroy you, deter you, or delay you from reaching your destiny! You can move from pain to power by the grace of our God!"[51]

Isaiah 41:10 – "Fear thou not; for I [am] with thee: be not dismayed; for I [am] thy God: I will strengthen thee; yea, I will help thee; yea, I will uphold thee with the right hand of my righteousness."

---

[51] *Sitting at lunch and talking about writing a book, my sister wanted me to share her story to empower women who are hurt by past, painful experiences. 6/2014.*

EPILOGUE

This book has been entitled *The Safety Pin*. My prayer for you is that by now you have discovered your own safety pin. At those times in your life when it seems that your internal world is crumbling, as your external world turns inside out, there is that something that God has given you to keep you grounded. There is that symbol that is filled with meaning and has relevance for your remaining steadfast. It may be a Scripture, a particular prayer, or a closet into which you retreat. May it be yours to treasure. Mine is the safety pin. As simple as it is, it brings tears to my eyes when it shows up in places that I am not expecting; on a desk, in a teller window, in a hotel room, on the sidewalk in front of a church, on the floor inside of a room where I train students. Yes, as simple and as trivial as it may seem to you, it is special to me.

A closing word about your purpose

In order that you might live fully the life that God has ordained for you, you must make it your personal mission to discover your purpose. You have one. One place to start is by asking yourself some questions. What is it that drives your passion that you would do even if you never got paid for it? What is that you do that gives you a sense of fulfillment? What is it that brings you to a stronger awareness of God?

The path toward your purpose might be discovered in four words of the Lord's Prayer: "Your will be done" (Matthew 6:10). Howard Thurman, my favorite mystic, says it best:

> It is the fundamental character of me. It is the foundation of my mental, physical and spiritual structure. It is what I find when I am most myself. It is what I find when I get down to the deepest things in me. It is what is revealed when all the superficial things are sloughed off and I am essentially laid bare."[52]

As you begin this journey of discovering your purpose, or even embracing what you know your purpose to be, may you yearn to lie bare before God until the light of Christ reveals to you who and what you were born to be. Walking in your purpose will be the easiest walk you have ever done. I learned my purpose a long time ago. It is that of a caregiver. My youngest brother Ronnie leaned heavily on me to take care of his hurts and pain. I remember one day he decided to walk across a hot pipe, not realizing how hot it was until he was too far to turn back. He dropped to his knees and crawled backwards off the pipe. He ran home to me. My mother was at work, so I made him lie down while I attended to his pain to make it better. I then gave him a spoon of water with sugar. Within minutes he claimed to feel better. When my mother took ill, I flew home to Georgia because I wanted to care for her, to listen to her story, to bathe her and to love

---

[52] Howard Thurman, *Deep is the Hunger* (Indiana: Friends United Press, 1951), 193.

on her. Before she died, she said to me, "I feel so much love from you." To this day, I value caring for others. It is a place where I feel whole.

My career is in caregiving. I love it so much that now I train others to be caregivers, and I also train others to do the kind of training that I so love. I don't see my job as work; I see it as fulfilling my purpose. When you discover your purpose, you will not see yourself doing anything other than what you are doing. My call to the gospel ministry is an act of caregiving. It is caring for the souls of people; caring about their experience of abundant life and ultimately, eternal life. My prayer for you is that you find time to be quiet before God and allow Him to reveal your purpose to you if you are not already living your purpose.

Perhaps you should partner with a sister within your church, on your job, or in your circle, and begin the journey toward the "naked self" without all the titles, the trappings, and the distractions of this world. Take that journey to gain deeper insight into the self. God will walk there with you. The psalmist took this journey and declared, "The Lord will fulfill His purpose for me; Your steadfast love, O Lord, endures forever. Do not forsake the work of Your hands" (Psalm 138:8).

This process of moving toward your purpose will constrain you to take your sister along with you. It will bring you to a new kind of intimacy with your sister. You are your sister's keeper. Walk with her. And finally, may this journey toward your purpose help you to identify or rediscover your safety pin!

42653201R00071

Made in the USA
Lexington, KY
30 June 2015